HEROES *of* AMERICA ™

ELEANOR ROOSEVELT

by **Shannon Donnelly**

illustrations by **Guy Wolek**

BARONET
BOOKS

BARONET BOOKS, New York, New York

HEROES OF AMERICA™

Edited by
Joshua Hanft and Rochelle Larkin

HEROES OF AMERICA™ is a series of dramatized lives of great Americans especially written for younger readers. We have selected men and women whose accomplishments and achievements can inspire children to set high goals for themselves and work with all of us for a better tomorrow.

Table of Contents

Important Dates

1884   Eleanor Roosevelt is born in New York

1892   Mother Anna dies

1894   Father Elliot dies

1899   Eleanor goes to school in England

1901   Uncle Theodore becomes president

1904   Eleanor and Franklin become engaged

1905   Eleanor marries Franklin

1921   Franklin crippled by polio

1932   Eleanor becomes First Lady of the United States

1944   Franklin re-elected president for fourth term

1945   Franklin dies

1945   Eleanor appointed to the United Nations

1962   Eleanor Roosevelt dies

Chapter 1

A Shy and Solemn Child

Eleanor tiptoed down the dark staircase in her grandmother's New York mansion. The sounds of horses and carriages did not pass through the thick velvet curtains and heavy doors. Eleanor did not want to be the one to make any noise. But it was hard for an eight-year-old girl, especially now—now when she wanted to run and cry and say it hadn't happened; not to her, not to her mother.

She glanced at the black ribbons tied to the polished wooden stair rail—black for her mother; black for the death of Anna Rebecca Livingston Ludlow Hall Roosevelt.

She Would Never Be as Pretty as Her Mother.

ELEANOR ROOSEVELT

Tugging on her mourning dress, Eleanor tried to make it fit better. She knew she would never be as pretty as her mother. She didn't have wide blue eyes and thick, gold hair and a soft, round face. No, she had eyes not quite blue, not quite gray, dark blond hair that wouldn't stay in a ribbon, and a long face with too wide a mouth. Eleanor wasn't pretty. But she still wanted to look nice for Father.

She only had her father left now . . . and her brothers.

She crossed the big silent hall, her shoes tapping on the wood floor. At the tall oak doors, she stopped. Her heart beat so fast it made her head spin. Would her father agree to take her with him? She wanted so much to travel with him, as the whole family did before. She breathed deeply and opened the door.

ELEANOR ROOSEVELT

Long brown curtains covered the windows, blocking the dim winter sunlight. Carriage wheels clattered outside, sounding as if they were miles away as they passed by. Her father, Elliott Roosevelt, sat in a high-backed chair beside an unlit fireplace. Everything he wore was black, except for his white shirt. He sat still, his face turned away. He almost disappeared into the gloom.

Looking up, he saw Eleanor and held out his arms. She ran across the room to him. For a very long time, she stood with her face pushed against his chest. The cold of the room pressed against her back.

"Nell . . . my little Nell . . ." he whispered; only he had ever called her Nell. Her mother had called her Granny because she didn't smile, and wasn't pretty. Eleanor hugged her father tighter.

He held her close. "Now I only have you and your brothers. Do you remember the photograph of you pointing your finger and scolding me?

Only He Had Ever Called Her Nell.

Scolding Father . . . You had a right to. I shall never be able to make up for not being with your mother during her illness. And now she's gone."

Eleanor turned her face to look at her father. "Can we go home now?"

"Darling Nell. I'm still too ill. I must keep traveling and looking for a cure. You have to live with Grandmother Hall. But you must never forget to write to me. Someday we shall travel together again as we used to. Remember how we once went to Venice and I sang to you on the canals as if I were your own gondolier? We shall have such fun again, my Nell."

Tears spilled down her face, wet and salty. "Father?"

He brushed away Eleanor's tears. "No crying," he said. "That's not for a Roosevelt. You must look after the little ones. You must not give your grandmother any trouble. Study hard and grow up into a fine woman, a woman to make me proud."

Eleanor nodded. Why couldn't she go with him now? She was big enough. And she could look after Elliott and Hall. They could all travel together.

"I shall see you as often as I can." He winked at her, as if sharing a secret.

Eleanor smiled a little. She wanted to show Father that she could be good right now—that he didn't have to wait to take her with him. But she knew it was no use. She had to look down and concentrate on his black pearl tie tack, so that she would not cry again.

He kissed her head. Then he left.

Eleanor stared at the empty doorway. She did not even hear the wheels of the carriage that took Father away again.

She felt so lonely. Grandmother Hall's house was very large—a mansion, really—but that made her feel even more lost. The fancy things around her didn't mean very much to a little girl. What did it matter that this house was

She Didn't Have Her Mother Any More.

big, or the curtains velvet, or that there were servants to do everything? Eleanor had no friends to play with, no cousins her own age to visit.

She hadn't minded all of this so much, before. But now, she didn't have her mother any more . . . her beautiful mother who had tried so hard to make Eleanor feel loved and wanted.

And now her father was gone again—the father she loved so much, but hardly ever saw. A big lump formed in her throat. She tried to swallow, but she couldn't. She tried to push away the tears that always came, but they came flooding out anyway.

Her whole body was shaking with sobs. She had to hold on to the carved wooden bannister as she made her way to her dark, quiet room.

"Dear Father," Eleanor said as she wrote down the words. Then she stopped, and chewed on the end of her pen.

She sat in Grandmother Hall's dining room at the back of the house. Spring sunlight shone in through the long windows. Outside a bird sang in the small garden behind the mansion.

Turning back to her letter, she started her next line. I *write to thank* . . . The ink smudged the "k" and Eleanor wrinkled her nose . . . . *to thank you for your kind note and to tell you how sorry I am to hear that Ellie is so sick.*

She stopped and looked at the letters. That spring, her brothers—Elliott and Hall—had both caught scarlet fever. They had both been sent to Grandmother's house in the country to get better. Hall was better. But Ellie had gotten even sicker. Now everyone talked in whispers, just as they had last fall before Mother went to live with the angels.

Sunshine Shone Through the Long Windows.

Pressing her lips together tightly, Eleanor wrote, *we must remember that Ellie is going to be safe in heaven and be with Mother* . . .

A tear smudged the next word. She blotted the smudge. Feeling all twisted up inside, she tried to be as brave as her father would want her to be. She wrote some more lines to make him feel better. Then she gave him her love, and signed the letter, *Nell*.

Tapping her heels against her chair, Eleanor glanced around the empty room. The house seemed so quiet again. She heard a clock chime. She sighed. When would Hall come back so she could look after him? When would Father come to take them home? Would she even have a real home, ever again?

In the summer, Eleanor went to stay with Hall at Grandmother's house in the country. Oak Terrace sat five miles up from a village called Tivoli. It took hours to travel there on the train from New York City. The big, square two-story house faced the Hudson River, and the opposite side looked out onto a garden. Around the house, the woods of the Hudson Valley made it seem like a stone castle in an enchanted forest.

In the winter, Grandmother took Eleanor and Hall back to New York, back to the big house on West 37th Street. Back to lessons with Mr. Roser, and lessons from French teachers, and governesses, and all sorts of people hired to look after Eleanor and Hall.

Then one day, Eleanor had a surprise.

"Mr. Elliott Roosevelt is here to see you," the butler announced.

Eleanor looked up from her studies. "Father?" Jumping up from her seat, Eleanor ran into the hall. At the stairs, she stopped. She knew a fast way down. Swinging a leg over the bannister, she slid down backward. She did not even see her father standing at the bottom of the stairs.

"We Shall Have an Outing Today!"

Instead, she fell right into him!

His silk hat flew into the air. He clutched her and staggered backward. Laughing, he caught her and swung her up. "I thought I was calling on a lady!" he said. "Who is this scamp?"

Eleanor threw her arms around his neck, squeezing tight.

He laughed. "Fetch your jacket and hat. We shall have an outing today!"

She ran back upstairs. It took only a moment to get her coat and a bonnet. She hurried down the stairs. Then, she forced herself to walk, not run, across the hall to the front doors.

Father asked about her studies as they strolled on the avenue. He wanted to know if she had gotten better at math. He asked her to speak to him in French. She held his hand and skipped beside him. She told him about how big Hall had grown, and how much she liked her piano lessons.

Her father took her to a building where some ragged boys were sitting on wooden benches. Eleanor was surprised that some of the boys did not even have shoes. She asked her father why not.

He looked down at her. "These boys are poor, Eleanor. Some do not even have a home. They sleep in wooden shacks on empty lots. Your grandfather—my father, Theodore—started this clubhouse to help these boys. To give them a place to learn. It is the obligation of anyone with money to help those without."

She blinked at him. "Do you help?"

He smiled sadly at her. "Yes, Eleanor. I can help others better than I help myself. And your mother used to do even more, with her charities and good works. There is such distress in the world. Even I have suffered from the recent financial setbacks in this country. But I can help a little here, and as a trustee of the Children's Aid Society."

Some of the Boys Did Not Even Have Shoes.

"Can I help?" Eleanor asked, wanting him to say yes.

His smile widened. "Would you like to help me serve Thanksgiving dinner here this year?"

She glanced at the thin-faced boys. One boy stared back, his face drawn and angry. Eleanor moved closer to her father, and glanced up at him. He looked at her, waiting for an answer. She pushed back her fear of the ragged boy and smiled. "Yes, I'd like that. I'd like to help."

Chapter 2

The Years at Tivoli

Eleanor sat in the big cherry tree behind her grandmother's house. The branch was big enough to hold her and Hall, but Hall was still too small to climb trees. Besides, this was her tree. Her secret place. Putting her book on her chest, she leaned back against the rough bark. Sunlight came through the leaves to tingle on her cheek.

She had only gotten one letter from Father this summer. *Darling Nell: What must you think of a father who has not written in so long? I have been ill, sometimes not able to move from my bed . . .*

Thinking about Father Being Ill

She bit her lip. She didn't want to think about Father being ill.

"El-la-norrrr." The long shout echoed in the garden. Eleanor sat up. Grandmother never called for her. Climbing down from the tree, Eleanor brushed the twigs and leaves from her dress. She ran to the house and found Grandmother standing on the stone terrace.

Grandmother Hall took Eleanor inside to the big library. Telling Eleanor to sit down, Grandmother perched on one of the straight-backed chairs. She sat, twisting the rings on one hand. What was wrong? Eleanor's throat went dry. Was she going to have to live with someone else?

"Eleanor—your father . . . it's a fearful shock . . . he died a few days ago."

"No!" Eleanor jumped up. "He just wrote me! No! No! It can't be!" Tears streamed down her face.

She spun away and ran upstairs to her room. Slamming the door, she threw herself onto her bed. She turned her face into the pillow and sobbed, her body quivering. Finally, she cried herself to sleep.

Eleanor woke the next morning, still in her dress. Wiping her face, she sat up. She stared at her room—the same room; the same wallpaper; the same big bed.

Only, nothing was the same. Father was gone.

Somehow the summer ended. Her birthday came and went. None of it seemed as real to her as the books she read.

Her governess, Madeleine, began to take the books away, saying that she was a stupid girl to live in dreams. So Eleanor had to hide her books. She woke early to read before breakfast. And she did not cry when Madeleine punished her for reading. She only wished that she was brave enough to tell Grandmother about how awful Madeleine was.

She Cried Herself to Sleep.

"Five, six, seven, eight, and feet in fourth position—to fifth position—arms, ladies! Do not flap them like goose wings!"

Eleanor struggled to point her toes out and lift her chest. In the long mirrors on the dance studio wall, sweat gleamed on her face. She gripped the wooden ballet bar more tightly.

Now that they were in New York City again for the winter, Eleanor attended a small ballet studio on Broadway once a week. Grandmother thought the lessons would help Eleanor stand straighter.

The other girls were all training for careers in the theater. After class, they laughed and talked of how they would dance on the stage. Eleanor wished she could join them. But Roosevelts did not become dancers, Grandmother said. So Eleanor practiced the steps, and pretended that she, too, would be in the spotlight someday.

"Child, can you not stand up any straighter?"

Grandmother Hall chided, shaking her head.

Eleanor pulled her shoulders back, then squirmed as muscles stiffened. She went to ballroom dancing class now that she was thirteen, to learn how to waltz and polka. On Mr. Dodsworth's polished parquet floor, Eleanor was taller than any boy in the dancing class, and it made her feel like a giraffe.

With bony fingers, Grandmother Hall felt Eleanor's back. "It must be a spinal curvature," she remarked. "Your mother walked four miles a day with a staff between her elbows and her back to give her perfect posture."

Eleanor lowered her eyes. Her grandmother tucked a finger under Eleanor's chin and lifted her face. "We must see a doctor."

The doctor put Eleanor into a steel brace. It was worse than the braces she had had to wear on her teeth. She didn't feel as if she

Everyone Bowed to Aunt Gracie.

could move in it, let alone ride her pony or her bicycle.

She hated her braces. Then one of her father's sisters, Aunt Gracie, took her to a hospital. "Your grandfather, Theodore Roosevelt, helped Dr. Schaefer start the Orthopedic Hospital," Aunt Gracie said as they stepped out of the carriage. "The family is still deeply involved with this hospital, and someday you may be as well."

Eleanor walked behind Aunt Gracie as the doctors showed them around. Everyone bowed to Aunt Gracie, hurrying to do anything she asked. Wandering down one of the halls by herself, Eleanor poked her head into a doorway and looked into a room that had beds lined up against two walls. There was a child in every bed. Each one had a leg, or an arm, in a cast or a splint. Near the doorway, one boy sat in a wheelchair. Steel braces gleamed on both of his legs. Eleanor walked over to him.

"Hello."

The boy looked up but he did not smile.

"I have to wear a brace, too." Eleanor tugged her shirt from her skirt and lifted it to show her back brace.

The boy's eyes brightened. "Does yours hurt?" he asked.

Eleanor nodded. "I have to wear it for a year."

The boy looked down at his legs. "I have to wear mine for always."

Eleanor no longer minded her back brace. She sat down beside the boy to talk to him. She was there still when her aunt came looking for her.

Eleanor began to make school friends. She still had lessons with Mr. Roser, but now the classroom moved to the homes of the other students, to Helen Cutting's house or Jessie Sloan's mansion. Eleanor liked Helen and Jessie. They didn't mind that she wore ugly high-button shoes and straight dresses with

"I Have to Wear a Brace, Too."

no shape. But the other girls, particularly Margaret Dix, liked to giggle in class and make fun of everyone.

Eleanor tried to listen to Mr. Roser's lessons. When Margaret held up her fingers with painted faces on every fingernail—and one looking a lot like Mr. Roser with his bushy whiskers and grim face—Eleanor tried not to laugh. The other girls muffled their giggles.

"Eleanor!"

Eleanor jumped and rose up out of her chair. "Yes, Mr. Roser?"

"Please come here. Young ladies, today you have a special treat. Miss Roosevelt—whose talents for composition and memorization are well-known to you, will recite Alfred, Lord Tennyson's poem, *The Revenge.*"

Her cheeks hot, Eleanor stood at the front of the room and stared at her classmates. Margaret rolled her eyes and slumped in her chair. Helen grinned. Jessie smiled and sat up.

Eleanor began. As she recited, Margaret made fun of the gestures Mr. Roser had taught them. Eleanor turned her head and flung out an arm. So did Margaret. Eleanor put her hand to her head at a sad moment. So did Margaret. But Margaret's antics could not make Eleanor forget the words.

She finished and Mr. Roser dismissed the class. Jessie and Helen came up to Eleanor to tell her how much they liked the recitation. "That was great, but when are you going to write another story?" Jessie demanded.

"I liked the one about the flowers who argued about who is the most beautiful," Helen said. "They're like us, equal but all in a special way. Even you, Eleanor. You aren't pretty, but boys look at you anyway. You catch the eye."

Eleanor felt her face blush. She didn't like to talk about boys. She couldn't believe any boy

"Ladies Do Not Run, Eleanor!"

would ever look at her. The boys in her dancing class certainly did their best not to.

"Well, I liked the story of the gilded butterflies who weren't happy with what they have," Margaret said, walking past them. "Some people just don't know when to settle for less."

Glaring at Margaret, Eleanor felt her fingers curl into a fist.

"Never mind her," Helen said. "I want you to ask your grandmother when you might come and stay with me again."

They made plans until their servants came to fetch them home. When Eleanor got home she ran upstairs. Grandmother looked up as Eleanor ran into the room. "How many times have I told you—ladies do not run, Eleanor!"

"Grandmother, please can I visit Helen Cutting this summer?"

Grandmother Hall shook her head. "You have other plans this summer. Uncle Teddy has asked, and I have agreed—you are to visit your father's family at Oyster Bay."

"Eleanor!" Uncle Teddy lifted Eleanor down from the carriage, crushing her in a hug. Uncle Teddy was a very strong man. He smelled of horses and salt air. His bristling mustache scratched her forehead and his arms closed around her like steel.

Eleanor felt happier than she had in a very long time. She was glad she didn't have to wear a brace on her back any more. Uncle Teddy might have snapped it. He set her down on her feet and turned to grab Hall from the carriage.

"Welcome to Sagamore Hill! We'll have a bully time now that my favorite niece and nephew are here. Hall, you grow to look more like your father every day. Oh, what memories you bring back!"

As they strode up to the house trying to keep up with his long strides, the children

Uncle Teddy Lifted Eleanor from the Carriage.

listened to Uncle Teddy talk about how he and their father used to ride and hunt and do everything together. "Your father was a real sportsman. Never was there such a brother!"

Uncle Teddy swept the children into his house. Inside, he handed Hall over to his son, Quentin. The two boys—both about the same age, Eleanor judged—stared at each other. Then Quentin asked if Hall would like to play. Hall nodded and the boys raced outside together.

"Capital!" Uncle Teddy exclaimed. He said "capital" a lot—and "bully" too, when he liked something. "Now, Eleanor, I shall see if Alice can't help you settle in. Alice!" he called.

Alice came running and jumping down the stairs. Eleanor watched her, shocked. But Uncle Teddy said nothing to Alice about acting like a lady. *How beautiful she is!* Eleanor thought to herself.

"Ah, Alice, you must show Eleanor around. Make her feel at home, can you? And we shall all go swimming this afternoon."

They all ate lunch in a huge dining room filled with food and talking and laughter. This house seemed bursting with children, with aunts and uncles. Aunt Edith, Teddy's wife, sat at one end of the table. Uncle Teddy sat at the other end, and his booming laugh nearly shook the crystal glasses.

After the meal, everyone went upstairs to change into swimming clothes. Eleanor had to borrow a swimming dress—she didn't even own one. Then Uncle Teddy, looking even bigger in his black tank-top and long swimming trunks, gathered everyone to walk down to the bay.

At the ocean, the boys dropped their towels and ran for the wooden dock. They jumped off the planks, splashing into the water, laughing and shoving. Uncle Teddy grinned and turned

"I Don't Know How to Swim."

to Eleanor. "What are you waiting for? Dive in!"

Eleanor bit her lower lip. She stood on one foot, and then the other. Then she stood on tiptoe and whispered to him, "I don't know how to swim."

Uncle Teddy grinned. "Just jump in, paddle and keep your head up!"

Alice jumped in and splashed with the boys. Turning, Quentin pushed Alice's head underwater. She came right back up, grabbing to push him under.

Swallowing, Eleanor glanced up at Uncle Teddy watching her. She thought of how her father had looked at her that same way, waiting for her to be brave. Taking a deep breath, she ran forward. Her feet slapped on the wooden planks. She held her nose, closed her eyes, and jumped.

The water seemed to swallow her, closing over her head. After the hot sun, she gasped at the coldness. A mouthful of salty water washed down her throat. She tried to cry out, but more water came in. Struggling, she paddled her arms. Sobbing in the water, she kicked her legs and she tried to climb back to the surface for air.

Her head came up and she gulped down a breath. Everyone laughed. Alice splashed over to her and pushed Eleanor's head under again. Panic gripped her. Her heart felt ready to burst. She needed air. She flung out her arms. Alice let go.

Eleanor bobbed up, arms wildly hitting the sea. Then a strong hand grabbed the back of her bathing dress. Her head came up above the salt water and she stared at Uncle Teddy's grin.

"Bully for you, Eleanor! That's it! A few hours and you'll be swimming like a duck!"

Eleanor pushed her swimming cap out of her eyes. She shivered. A few hours suddenly

"Bully for You, Eleanor!"

seemed like a very, very long time. She struggled back to where her feet touched the sand and she stayed there without budging.

Eventually, Uncle Teddy led everyone back to the house. Eleanor hugged her towel around her. The sand felt warm between her toes.

That night, Uncle Teddy built a bonfire in the backyard. In the orange glow of the flames, he told stories about his expeditions hunting buffalo and lions. As he talked, he snarled and pawed the ground and acted out all the roles in his stories. When he finished telling about his own, he pulled out a book and read even more stories of great adventure. Eleanor sat listening to him, happy and tired. She fell asleep that night dreaming of faraway lands.

Sunday ended with a party. Eleanor did not enjoy the dancing. Even with all her lessons she did not dance well. She was too tall, too gawky. But she liked the music. She found a quiet corner where no one could see her and sat behind a potted palm, listening to the records on Uncle Teddy's new record player.

A booming voice made her jump. "There you are!" Uncle Teddy strode across the floor in his fancy black coat and trousers. "We're going to play charades. And I want you on my team, you clever girl."

Grasping her hand, he pulled her to her feet. He grinned down at her and then he caught her in one of his huge bear hugs.

After that, Eleanor and Hall visited Sagamore Hill every summer. She learned to stay in the shallow water when she swam and she hoped that no one ever saw how frightened she was. But she liked it best when they went camping for the weekend. She could do that.

Rain chased the Roosevelt cousins back to the house one day in the summer of 1898. They brought in their wet tents and climbed the stairs to Uncle Teddy's gunroom. He read stories to them, and he talked about Cuba. There,

A Family Christmas Party

he told how he and his Rough Riders had fought to make Cuba an independent nation.

That Christmas, Grandmother Hall also allowed Eleanor go to a family party in New York. Glancing around the room filled with bright decorations, Eleanor decided she would have liked the party more if she had had a dress like Alice's,—a dress with lace ruffles around the neck and blue ribbons.

Eleanor looked down at her own dress. It had no ribbons, no lace. Grandmother Hall didn't see why little girls needed those things—only, Eleanor wasn't little. She had turned fourteen that October.

She stared at her shoes. Then she remembered Grandmother's orders and straightened her head, only to see a boy standing in front of her. Her mouth dropped open. He was actually two inches taller than she was.

"Hello, you're Eleanor, aren't you? Elliott's daughter? You don't remember, but we met before."

Eleanor's mind raced. She felt dizzy. How could she have met him and not remember him? She didn't know all that many boys. Who was he?

And what in the world was she going to say to him, whoever he was?

Who Was He?

Chapter 3

Changes Come

Eleanor stared at the boy. His smile widened. "When you were two, you rode on my back around the nursery at my mother's. Of course, I don't remember, either. I was only four."

"Then how do you know that it happened?" she asked.

"My mother told me." He pointed to a woman sitting in a chair, watching him. "She's Sara Delano Roosevelt. Do you find it difficult, being a Roosevelt? So many cousins. I've met a dozen new ones just tonight." He smiled again.

She smiled back, and mumbled, "I'm proud to be a Roosevelt."

"Are you? Then so am I. What do you want to do when you grow up? I'll probably go to law school. My father's a lawyer. But I wouldn't mind following Uncle Teddy into politics. Now that's exciting work."

Eleanor glanced up at his sparking eyes. "I suppose I . . . I don't know what I'll do."

"Don't you have any ambition?"

"Of course I do. I wrote an essay on ambition. Mr. Roser thought it was worth publishing."

"What did you write? Can you remember any of it?" he asked, a challenge in his deep voice.

She met his stare. Eleanor could remember almost everything she ever had read or written. "It is easier to have no ambition and just keep on the same way every day and never try to do grand and great things," she began,

Now He Would Make Fun of Her.

quoting every word. "But those with ambition try again—and try until they at last succeed."

She let the words die away. The music ended. The young man turned and clapped. Everyone clapped for the band.

Eleanor stared at the floor, face flaming. Now he would make fun of her, as Margaret Dix had in class.

"You have a very good mind, Miss Eleanor Roosevelt," he said, sounding surprised. He grinned. "Now, would you like some punch?"

They talked for some time and Eleanor forgot to feel shy or gawky. He had the gift of laughter. He said silly, teasing things. But he never asked stupid questions like the other boys. After he left, Eleanor turned to find Alice next to her. Alice leaned close to Eleanor. "I can't believe you spent all that time with Feather Duster," she said.

"Who?" Eleanor asked.

"F.D.! Feather Duster. It's what we call him. He's as light as one. Such a mama's boy." Alice fluffed the lace on her dress, proudly.

Eleanor's face went hot again, but not for herself this time. "He was nice. I liked him," she told Alice.

Alice stared at her. Then her blue eyes turned to ice. "You don't even know who he is."

"He's a Roosevelt," Eleanor said, thinking of the family names she had learned over the years. "His name is Franklin. Franklin Delano Roosevelt."

Eleanor woke early and lay in bed. She wiggled her toes in the sheets. Summer's hot days had come, leaving Oak Terrace shady and cool only inside. Stretching, Eleanor glanced at her clock. She had a little time before she had to get up. She reached under her mattress and pulled out *Ivanhoe.* She would just read a few pages.

She read more than a few pages. She read a whole chapter. When a sharp knock rapped on

"Feather Duster. It's What We Call Him."

her door, Eleanor slid down under the sheets. Madeleine, the housekeeper, pushed opened the door.

"What is this?" Madeleine strode across the room and snatched the book. "You are not supposed to read before breakfast!"

Eating in silence, Eleanor listened to Hall ask Grandmother silly questions about what Uncle Teddy did in politics. Grandmother answered all his questions. Then she asked Eleanor to walk with her in the garden.

"Are you happy?" Grandmother asked as they walked. "You've had so few friends. I worry sometimes that I've not done enough."

Eleanor hopped a step, pulling at one itchy black stocking that kept falling down. She wasn't unhappy. She had a pony and a puppy, and Hall and Grandmother, and her school friends in the winter.

"You looked so sad this morning," Grandmother said.

ELEANOR ROOSEVELT

Staring at the dew on the grass, Eleanor thought of Madeleine. She didn't mean to say anything. She only opened her mouth and suddenly the words spilled out like water from a broken glass. Grandmother Hall walked beside her, frowning. Finally, Eleanor stopped talking. Would Grandmother punish her for not being good enough to please Madeleine?

"Child, why didn't you tell me this before?"

Eleanor hung her head. It sounded so silly now to say that Madeleine frightened her.

"Well, I think it is time for a change," Grandmother went on. "You're fifteen. And your mother wanted you to go to boarding school in Europe."

"Europe?" Eleanor grabbed her grandmother's wrinkled hand. "Oh, Grandmother, I've always wanted to travel! But who will take me? Can I have a new dress? When do I go?" She had a million questions. Nothing this exciting had ever happened to her before.

Eleanor Sailed from New York.

ELEANOR ROOSEVELT

A few months later, Eleanor sailed from New York with one of her aunts. On the ship, people waved handkerchiefs. Eleanor waved her arm frantically, but she couldn't see her grandmother waving from the pier. A stream of tears blurred everything.

Once in England, they took a train to London. Mouth open, Eleanor leaned out of the window to stare at the great stone buildings and the new automobiles that so frightened the horses. The next day, they traveled to her school, Allenswood.

Mademoiselle Souvestre greeted them, a French accent shaping her words. She was the headmistress of Allenswood. Her white hair waved back into a twist, framing her sharp face. Her dark eyes sparkled with curiosity. "So this is Eleanor? Your father's sister was one of my favorite students. Now, Signorina Samaia shall show you to your room while your aunt and I take tea."

As Eleanor walked down the hall, the Signorina told her Allenswood's rules. "You will speak French. I will instruct you in Italian. Lessons cover German, mathematics, history, literature, philosophy, music, and the arts. Exercise is mandatory—a walk after breakfast and two hours each afternoon. We dress for dinner."

The Signorina stopped and opened a door. Inside the room, another girl looked up as she closed a thick book. "This is Marjorie Bennett," the Signorina said. "Marjorie, Eleanor is your roommate."

After the Signorina left, Marjorie gave Eleanor a shy smile. Eleanor liked her at once.

"Don't mind the Signorina, she's really a dear. Have you met Mademoiselle Souvestre? She can be harsh. But she's never unfair. Did you leave your bag downstairs? I'll bring it up. You must call me Bennett. That's what all the girls call me."

The Signorina Told Her Allenswood's Rules.

Eleanor changed into the school uniform that afternoon. Standing before a mirror, she smoothed the dark skirt. She liked the white shirt and the striped tie—just like a man's tie. On her bed lay her new blazer and a flat straw hat. She smiled, then wrinkled her nose. Her teeth still pushed forward, but at least her legs no longer seemed to stick out.

She went down to dinner with Bennett. They sat at long tables with thirty other girls, some struggling to speak French.

"The head table is for Mademoiselle and her teachers," Bennett said, leaning closer, "and the smartest girls in the school."

Watching the other girls seated next to Mademoiselle Souvestre, Eleanor suddenly wanted very much to be sitting there, too. All the girls looked so sure of themselves, so . . . so elegant.

Eleanor's days fell into a routine. Breakfast, a morning walk, and then classes. In the afternoon, she had field hockey practice, then more lessons before bedtime. She liked playing hockey on the soft English lawns. She wasn't good at games, but she started to wish that she was good enough at hockey to be on the best team—the first team.

"Eleanor," Mademoiselle Souvestre said, a few months after Eleanor had arrived, "I would like you to sit at my table tonight."

A smile swelled up inside Eleanor. "Of course, Mademoiselle."

When she told Bennett of this, the other girl hugged her. "I knew it wouldn't be long," Bennett said.

At dinner that evening, one girl looked miserable. When anyone asked her anything, she stumbled to answer in French. Eleanor tried to help. She whispered the right French words to the girl. And she asked Mademoiselle Souvestre a lot of questions about American history.

Eleanor Was Late to the Hockey Field.

After dinner, Mademoiselle Souvestre came over to Eleanor. "You have the warmest heart," she said. "Did you think I did not see how you helped the other girl at dinner? You would make a good teacher."

Eleanor went to bed, thoughts whirling in her head about becoming a teacher someday.

The next day, Eleanor was late to the hockey field. She had been writing a paper and forgot the time. She ran outside, puffing out clouds of warm breath in the cold air. "Have they said who made the first team yet?" Eleanor asked.

Bennett shook her head.

Then the games teacher strode out onto the grass, a clipboard in one hand. "Well, girls," she declared. "You all worked very hard."

Eleanor closed her eyes tightly. She tried very hard not to want this.

"Girls on the first team—Eleanor . . ."

Blinking, Eleanor opened her eyes.

"Well done!" Bennett said, gripping Eleanor's hand. Pride swelled in Eleanor's chest. She had done it. She had made the first team. For the first time in her life, she knew what it felt like to belong someplace.

The next year passed quickly. Eleanor worked hard at her lessons. She hated math. She liked to write essays, and learn new languages. At Allenswood, she celebrated the New Year, and a new century. 1900. It looked very odd when she had to write the numbers in her journal.

Spring arrived and Mademoiselle Souvestre asked Eleanor if she would like to travel to Florence, Italy, for the summer. "Your grandmother has agreed that you might come with me, if you like."

Eleanor could not stop the wide smile that burst onto her face. "If I . . . ? When do we start?"

Laughing, Mademoiselle Souvestre gave Eleanor a guidebook. "As soon as you arrange our timetable. Can you do that?"

For the First Time, She Felt She Belonged.

Hands shaking, Eleanor took the book. If Mademoiselle Souvestre thought she could do this, then she must.

They took the train to London and then to Dover. Eleanor found their bags and saw them carried to a ship, which crossed the English Channel. They traveled to Paris, and then south to Marseilles, and finally they took a train east, along the Mediterranean coast.

When they reached Florence, Mademoiselle Souvestre settled them at a friend's villa. "The only way to know a city is to walk it," she told Eleanor, "but it would exhaust me. So go and see Florence."

"Shouldn't I have someone with me? I'm only sixteen," Eleanor protested.

"Only sixteen? Victoria was only eighteen when she became Queen of England. Go. See the city. Enjoy your youth."

Grabbing her hat, Eleanor ran for the door,

skipping every other step. She had always wanted to go where she wanted and do what she wanted. Now she had a whole day—a day for adventure.

She got lost in narrow, cobbled streets. She bought her own lunch. She walked down to the Arno River. She fed fat gray pigeons in the big squares. She ate delicious ices and gawked at shop windows. She stopped in every church to look at the beautiful paintings.

Standing in front of the fountains of the Palazzo Vecchio, Eleanor stared at what had been the home of Italy's kings. The afternoon light cast rosy shadows on the old palace. Eleanor spread out her arms and tilted her head back, breathing in the fragrant air. She knew she would never be the same person again. She would cherish this moment inside her forever.

The next January, Eleanor got to travel again when she went to London for Queen

Eleanor Watched the Royal Funeral Parade.

Victoria's funeral. Her grandmother arranged for her to make the trip, and Mademoiselle Souvestre said, "You must go. You shall see history."

Outside her London hotel, Eleanor watched the royal funeral parade and thought about a girl who had become the monarch of a nation at only eighteen. Carriage after carriage slowly passed by. The horses' hooves clattered on the pavement. Royal guards on horseback rode down the street, red uniforms bright against all the black clothing in the crowd.

"Eighty-one years old, and sixty-three of those on the throne. I'd say that's a good run," said a man behind Eleanor. Someone hushed him. "Nothing to hush about. It's 1901! New year, new century, time for new faces," the man went on.

Eleanor turned to see a woman tug the man away. Then Eleanor looked back to watch the procession. Handkerchiefs fluttered as people wiped their eyes. Men took off their hats as the Queen's coffin rolled past. One person— one small woman—and yet so many cried for her passing.

When Eleanor got back to Allenswood, she found Bennett waiting for her, wanting to know all about the funeral.

"Do you think anyone will remember anything we do in our lives?" Bennett asked. She sat on her bed, arms clasped around her knees. "Don't you want to do something that makes you famous, something that lasts forever?"

Eleanor hung up her coat in the closet and then turned to Bennett. "All I want to do is something useful."

"Something useful? But don't you want a career?"

Eleanor walked over to the window. She stared out at the gray winter clouds. "I just want to do something useful. That's what makes me happy—being useful."

"I Want to Do Something Useful."

ELEANOR ROOSEVELT

Every week, Eleanor wrote to her grandmother, and to her brother, Hall. She ended each letter to Grandmother with a hint that she wanted to stay for a fourth year at Allenswood. But Grandmother Hall wrote back about the plans for Eleanor to "come out" the next fall. In Eleanor's day, young girls from prominent families were introduced into society at fancy parties. People called it "coming out."

Eleanor knew that her mother, Anna, had come out at eighteen. Every well-to-do girl did. Now she was expected to. That meant going to balls and parties, and meeting dozens of people who had known her mother. And all those people would stare and whisper, "She doesn't look like her mother. Her mother was pretty."

Eleanor thought about what Mademoiselle Souvestre had said when she heard that Eleanor must go. "Ah, what a blank your going must leave." Eleanor pressed her hand against the cold window. She felt like that inside: cold. All her plans to stay at Allenswood, to teach—for how long would she have to put them away?

New York Had Grown Up.

Chapter 4

Coming Out

New York had grown up. Electric streetcars clattered past. Noisy automobiles sped by. People hurried places. Sitting on a streetcar, Eleanor watched the bustle. She noticed a tattered man next to a woman on the street corner. Then a shriek split the air.

"Stop! Stop, thief!"

The ragged man ran down the street, a handbag dangling from his fingers. He glanced back. For a second, his wild gaze met Eleanor's stare. Fear rushed into her. The thief darted away, then he turned and disappeared around the corner.

The streetcar bell clanged. The car moved forward. Eleanor's fear faded. Next to her, a woman remarked about the nasty thief. Eleanor could only remember the frightened, hungry look in his eyes, and his ragged clothes. *People shouldn't have to live like that,* she thought. She remembered what her father used to say about privileged people helping others. Well, she might have to go to parties, but maybe she could still find ways to be useful.

"Cousin Susie, I can't fasten my gloves!" Eleanor held up the long white gloves that she was supposed to wear to the Assembly ball. Her fingers fumbled with the tiny buttons at her wrists.

Cousin Susie came over to help button the gloves. "Eleanor," she said, "What will people think of you if you stand shaking like a tall maple tree in a wind?"

She couldn't tell Cousin Susie that her hands shook because she hated these parties.

"I Can't Fasten My Gloves!"

She just wanted to go and get it over with. She didn't know anyone. Oh, Cousin Alice would be there with a dozen boys standing around her. Alice said things that made the boys laugh. Eleanor didn't know how to make anyone laugh.

Eleanor stared at her dress in the mirror; all lace and white silk fabric. It looked fit for a princess. The newspapers called Cousin Alice a princess.

Uncle Teddy had become President of the United States that September when a man shot and killed poor President McKinley. Now, everyone called Uncle Teddy, "Mr. President." They called his daughter Princess Alice.

And now they called Eleanor the niece of the president.

"Hold still," Cousin Susie commanded. "Now, remember, if you cannot think what to say to someone, just go through the alphabet. A? Do you like *Apples,* Mrs. Whitney? B?

Are you afraid of *Bears,* Mrs. Reid? People love to talk about themselves, so let them."

Eleanor pasted her best smile in place and pulled her shoulders back, ready for another long evening.

That weekend Eleanor escaped the endless social life of New York to visit Hall at his boarding school, Groton. She left the house and caught the train to the Boston area, away from New York and all those fancy, boring parties.

Hall seemed so much taller. Eleanor asked him about his classes and if he had made friends. He skipped along, shy now about holding her hand, but smiling and happy. Too soon, she had to leave to catch her train back to New York.

"You'll write, Totty, won't you?" Hall asked, his smile fading. He always called her that, since he was a baby.

"What a Surprise!"

She ruffled his gold hair. "Don't I always? And I'll come visit you soon again. Promise."

When she got on the train, the sense of loneliness crept up on her. When would she ever have her own home? Tivoli seemed like a memory now. Oak Terrace wasn't home, not with Hall away at school. But would she ever find a place for herself and Hall?

A cheerful male voice broke into her gloomy thoughts. "Cousin Eleanor? What a surprise!"

Turning, Eleanor glanced up into Franklin Roosevelt's twinkling grayish-blue eyes. She smiled at him and got up to shake his hand.

"Not so little any more, are you?" he said warmly, stepping closer so that she had to look up to see him. "I think I'm still an inch or two ahead. What are you doing here?"

Eleanor explained that she had traveled to Groton to see her brother.

"Groton? That's my old school. I'm next door, almost, at Harvard. Studying law." He made a face at her, his straight nose wrinkling and the lines creasing around his eyes.

"You don't want to study law?" Eleanor asked, surprised.

Franklin shrugged, then grinned. "What I want is for you to come and meet Mother. You must tell us about your trips. I heard something about your wanting to go back to England and be a teacher."

"How did you hear that?" She had only told Grandmother about that wish.

"Your grandmother told her daughter, who told my aunt, who told my mother, who told . . ."

Eleanor laughed. "I should have just put an ad in the newspaper!"

Grinning, Franklin led Eleanor into another train compartment. An older woman dressed in black looked up. Sara Delano Roosevelt looked like a queen. Back straight, hair touched by silver, she stared piercingly at Eleanor with raised eyebrows. Eleanor

She Stared Piercingly at Eleanor.

suddenly felt seven years old, as if facing her own mother after she had done something bad.

"Look whom I found, Mother! Cousin Eleanor. I thought she'd like to sit with us," Franklin said, his voice easy.

With a tight smile, Mrs. Roosevelt nodded. Eleanor let out a breath and sat down. She held her purse with both hands and nervously fiddled with the clasp as she talked to Franklin and his mother.

Franklin laughed when Eleanor told him she didn't like parties. Then he said, "But you have to go to Uncle Teddy's Inaugural Ball this March. I'll take you, so that way you'll have to enjoy it!"

Eleanor stared at the soft gas lighting in the White House, and at the crowds. Uncle Teddy had nearly invited the world to the ball that marked his being sworn in as president. And the world had come. Ambassadors. Kings.

Queens. Heads of states and people in exotic dress.

Pushing through the crowd, Franklin came back with two glasses of punch. "Wonderful, isn't it?" he said to Eleanor, almost shouting over the loud music and noise.

Wonderful? The excitement tingled on her skin and sparkled in her like bubbles. Imagine a president's inauguration; her uncle's inauguration. She felt very important. She said so to Franklin.

He frowned at her. "You're always important. Everyone's important. Look, there's Uncle Teddy. We must give him our best."

They shouldered past the other guests. Uncle Teddy grinned and reached out to hug Eleanor. "Ah, my little Eleanor!" He squeezed her shoulder so hard that it hurt. "You're the belle of my ball! I'm glad you don't put on airs like some of these modern girls."

Eleanor frowned. If she wasn't modern, did that make her old-fashioned? She thought of

He Spun Her Away to Dance.

how her mother had called her Granny. Inside her satin dress, Eleanor squirmed.

Uncle Teddy grinned. 'You're not like those silly Junior League girls who try to get their names into the papers with their parties! Now I must go and be nice to that horrible man who's the German ambassador." He patted Franklin's back heartily and moved toward the other guests.

Watching her uncle smile and pump the hand of the German ambassador, Eleanor asked, "Franklin, what's the Junior League?"

"Some charity group in New York. They do work for the poor. But enough talk. We're in the White House where Lincoln danced with Mary Todd. And we're here—just think of it!" Grinning, he took her punch glass and put it down, and spun her away to dance.

As soon as she got back to New York, Eleanor met with some other girls who worked with the Junior League. She and

Jean Reid would run a dance class at the Rivington Street Settlement. Eleanor liked the idea of a class that would give poor children some fun.

Eleanor took the streetcar to teach her first class. As she got closer to the poorer neighborhoods, the streets became dirty and narrow. Men in torn coats leaned against brick buildings or slumped in doorways. Even the buildings seemed shabby and worn. Watching the streets change, Eleanor sank in her seat and wondered if this had been such a good idea. She hurried to the address on Rivington.

Stepping into the gymnasium, Eleanor looked at the class. Twenty children, some in rags and some without shoes, shouted and ran wildly around the room. She almost walked out again. Then one child turned and stared at her. Within two seconds, some other children had turned to stare. Noise disappeared. Soon,

The Streets Became Narrow and Dirty.

twenty pairs of hungry eyes stared silently at Eleanor from gaunt faces.

Jean Reid came and helped Eleanor line up the children and start the class. Jean played the piano and Eleanor taught them the dances she knew. She asked Jean to play the new "ragtime" music. She had seen young people dancing the cakewalk where boys and girls walked with stiff legs and arms. The children liked that.

In a few minutes, Eleanor had the children dancing and laughing. She forgot about the shabby buildings and the children's dirty clothes. And the children's smiles were better than any party.

"You do what? Teach dancing to slum children?" Franklin asked later on.

They were sitting near the windows of his home in Hyde Park. Around them, music blared and the party for Franklin's twenty-first birthday swirled past.

Eleanor lifted her chin. Then she saw the sparkle in Franklin's eyes and knew that he was teasing. "And sometimes sewing," she said, still feeling that he didn't think her work important. "But I don't like that as much."

He laughed. "So that's what you've been doing since Uncle Teddy's Inaugural ball?"

"Well, I haven't had time for parties. I joined the Consumers League as well. Our goal is equal pay for equal work—for women, too. And a ten-hour workday at a good wage of six dollars a week. You should see how some factories keep children sitting at tables, working until they drop . . ." She broke off, looking at him from the corner of her eye. "Now, you're going to laugh at me."

He smiled. "No. I won't laugh. I've seen some of the same things. It's one thing I admire Uncle Teddy for. He at least tries to help. But there's so much to do."

"All the Little Girls Will Fall in Love with You."

"I know. Sometimes I could almost scream because I want to do so many things and can't! I'm still waiting for my life to start."

"Now, you do sound too serious." He smiled at her. "Would you mind if I came to watch your dance class some afternoon?"

Eleanor smiled. "You'll only make fun of me. And you'll make all the little girls fall in love with you."

"Of course I'll make fun of you. I like to see you smile. And it's only fair. You have all the boys in love with you."

Eleanor laughed at that.

Franklin didn't laugh. He looked at her, and shook his head. "You don't even know how many boys admire you."

Face hot, she laughed again. He had to be teasing her.

One crisp fall afternoon, Franklin came as he had said he would. Eleanor had been trying to teach the children how to do the fox-trot.

Jean pounded out a four-quarter rhythm on the upright piano. Stiff and frowning, the children stumbled over each other's feet.

"Am I interrupting?" Franklin said, poking his head into the room.

Everyone turned. Grinning, he strode in. He looked as if he came to the New York slums every day. Eleanor watched him, thinking how he always looked so confident.

Franklin smiled at the children, who seemed shy of him. Taking off his coat and hat, he put them on a chair. "What are you teaching? The two-step?"

"No. A fox-trot."

"Oh, but that's not how it's done. Shall we show them?" He grinned at Jean and nodded to her, then swept Eleanor up. Jean started playing.

"Now, how does this go? Left foot, right foot?" He pretended to stumble along.

"Am I Interrupting?"

Eleanor didn't know whether to laugh or step on his toes for acting so silly.

As Franklin spun her around, the children giggled. Franklin didn't quite step on her feet. "Come on," he said, turning to the children. "If you help me count my steps, I may get better. One, two, three, four, left, right, left, right."

Shyly, two of the boys started counting. Franklin straightened and started dancing better. "That's right. Now I'm getting it."

Giggling, the other children started counting. By the time the song ended, Franklin had danced Eleanor around the gym.

As the music ended, the children swarmed forward, curious about this stranger with the warm smile. He pulled their noses, asked them silly questions and sat down on the floor with them. Eleanor watched, amazed at how quickly they took to Franklin.

"Come on, let's try another dance," he said, getting up. Jean started a new song. Franklin helped Eleanor teach. Laughter and music soon filled the bare room. The afternoon slipped past.

After sending the children home, Eleanor turned to Franklin. "Thank you," she told him. "I don't think they've ever had such fun."

He grinned at her. "I don't think I have either."

Jean hurried forward, pulling on her coat. "Eleanor, are you sure you don't want to ride home with me?" She glanced at Franklin and smiled. "She never does ride home with me, but I have to ask. Honestly, Eleanor, I don't know how you are brave enough to ride the streetcars home at night."

"You take the streetcars?" Franklin asked.

Eleanor lifted her chin proudly. "Yes. Why shouldn't I?"

"Oh, you should. It's a terrible waste of money not to. But can I see you home, Eleanor?" Franklin asked, putting on his hat.

Franklin Showed Hall the Plays.

ELEANOR ROOSEVELT

As they walked outside into the brisk November air, he turned to her. "Eleanor, would you come to the Harvard-Yale football game? I mean, well, I'd like you to come. I'm leading the cheers."

Eleanor looked at him. For an instant Franklin looked so serious; then his grin reappeared. She liked that about him. He always made life fun. "Of course I'll come," she said.

Eleanor took the train up to see the game, and the next day they both went to Groton to see Hall. The cold weather didn't stop Franklin and Hall from stripping off their coats so that Franklin could show Hall all the exciting plays of the football game.

After lunch they took Hall back to his school, then walked along the river toward the train station.

"Eleanor, I have something I've wanted to ask you for a long time," Franklin said solemnly, turning to stare at the icy river.

ELEANOR ROOSEVELT

She looked at him. Her heart beat fast. Was she waiting for something? Only . . . no, she couldn't hope for that. Hadn't everyone always told her that no young man would ever be interested in her—that she wasn't pretty enough.

"Next year, I graduate from Harvard," Franklin went on. "I'll probably go on to Columbia until I pass the bar exam and become a lawyer. And it's got me thinking about the future. And . . . well, what I want to know is if you'll marry me?"

Franklin grinned, confident as ever.

Eleanor stood still, heart fluttering, frozen. How could he be so sure? She knew what she wanted, but how could Franklin know?

His grin faded. He took her hands. "I have only a few bright prospects now, I know—but I'm sure I'll amount to something, with your help."

Surprised, Eleanor stared at Franklin. "Me? But I'm plain. I haven't much to bring you."

"...If You'll Marry Me?"

ELEANOR ROOSEVELT

"You have much more to bring me than you know. Now, will you? Eleanor—please say you will?"

For a moment, she couldn't say anything. All she had never even let herself hope for, or dream about, was coming true. She held her breath, not trusting herself to speak, afraid her voice wouldn't be able to say the words she wanted so much to say.

She felt Franklin looking closely at her. He was waiting for her answer.

She could only manage a whisper. But a whisper was enough. "Yes," she said, "Yes, I will!"

Chapter 5

A Political Life

Alice Roosevelt spread the train of Eleanor's wedding gown into a spill of white satin. "Oh, Eleanor, you're a saint to have me as your bridesmaid. But can anyone even get to your aunt's house today? I mean, New York on March 17th is the St. Patrick's Day parade."

Putting a hand over her stomach, Eleanor peeked into the other room. She could just see Franklin at the far end. They had waited a year to announce their engagement, and then set the date for March 17, 1905. Mother Roosevelt still did not seem happy about it.

"Keeping the Name in the Family," He Said.

Eleanor knew that Mrs. Roosevelt thought her son could do better.

The ceremony passed in a blur of words and cold, shaking hands. Franklin kissed her, people clapped and Uncle Teddy stepped forward.

"Nothing like keeping the name in the family," he said, grinning.

Uncle Teddy moved aside and most of the guests moved with him, in awe of the President. Eleanor's smile faded. This seemed more Uncle Teddy's party than her own wedding. The newspapers had been full of the President's niece getting married. She had even been mistaken for Alice by a reporter who asked if the wedding would be in the White House.

But Eleanor was married now. And now perhaps she might have her own home. A home for her, and for Hall when he came back from school.

They had to wait until June for Franklin to finish his spring term at Columbia law school before they went on a honeymoon.

"Well, what shall we do in Europe?" Franklin asked her. They walked the deck of the *Oceanic* as they sailed to Europe.

No one had ever asked Eleanor what she wanted to do. "Can we shop? And eat out? I want to try everything. And can we sit at one of the little tables on the Piazza San Marco in Venice and feed the pigeons? I did that when my parents brought me to Europe."

"When you were a baby?" He tucked her hand into the crook of his arm. "Well, you're my baby now. My Babs!" Franklin always called her Babs.

In Venice, Franklin hired a gondolier who looked like a bandit and who sang as he rowed them out onto the canals. And in Scotland they bought a black Scottish terrier that Franklin christened Duffy.

Franklin Hired a Gondolier.

Eleanor felt awful on the ocean voyage home. She had never been so ill before and she tried to hide her sickness. Finally, though, she went to the ship's doctor. She was going to have a baby!

The following May of 1906, Eleanor had her first child, a girl.

Lying in bed, Eleanor held the small, wiggling Anna. With a pudgy red face, little Anna did not look like any doll Eleanor had ever played with. And she wiggled so much! When Anna whimpered, Eleanor looked helplessly at the nurse. "What is it? What's wrong with her?"

The nurse smiled. "Oh, she's just wants her lunch. You'll learn what to do. You're her mother."

Anna's tiny hand batted out and her little fingers closed over Eleanor's nightgown, clutching tight. Eleanor wanted suddenly so much to do everything right for this tiny little girl.

ELEANOR ROOSEVELT

She looked up as Franklin strode into the room smiling, a newspaper in his hands. "Did you see this? Uncle Teddy won the Nobel Peace Prize for ending the war between the Russians and Japanese!"

"Oh, how wonderful!" Eleanor said, sitting up too quickly. Baby Anna began to cry.

Franklin laughed and tickled his daughter's cheek. "Well, here's one Roosevelt who doesn't like politics."

In December of the next year, another baby came, a son, James, named after Franklin's father. Eleanor did not feel well after the baby was born, and the nurse had to look after both James and little Anna. Franklin passed his law exams and became a lawyer on Wall Street. The four of them moved into a house built for them by Franklin's mother.

Walking into the narrow building, Eleanor stared at the house that her mother-in-law had bought and decorated. Would she ever

Eleanor Stayed Busy with Her Babies.

have her own house—a house *she* made for herself and her family?

Eleanor stayed busy with her babies. She tried so hard to be a good mother, but somehow she always felt as if she had not done enough. She wanted to love and cuddle these tiny little ones, but all the books said that babies should be left in their cribs. It all seemed so hard. Eleanor rode horses sometimes in Central Park and played golf for exercise, but she felt as if she were drifting. And she didn't know quite where she fit in—not even in her own family.

"Well, Uncle Teddy is not going to run for reelection. It's such a shame," Franklin said as he sat down in a chair, looking tired.

Eleanor sat in Franklin's library with Anna on her lap and James in a crib. "He's been in office for seven years," she answered. "Surely that's enough."

"But why, when so many people don't have work, or have to work too hard just to keep their jobs?"

Eleanor smiled. "You may have to start working harder soon," she said. "I'm going to have another baby. And if it's a boy, I want to call him Franklin."

Franklin Junior was born the next year, in March. He was the biggest of the three babies, Eleanor thought as she held him. But he fussed so much. And he was so pale. She worried and tried so hard to take care of him. That winter, he became ill.

"It's his heart," the doctor said.

Eleanor gripped the crib railing. Tears choked her throat. But she wouldn't let them out. "Can't you do anything?"

The doctor shook his head and put away his medical bag.

Eleanor stared down at her baby. What would she ever do without him?

Standing by the tiny stone marker in the churchyard, Eleanor shivered. Franklin had only asked a few people to the funeral. A cold

Eleanor Gripped the Crib Railing.

wind pulled at her hat and coat. It seemed so hard to leave baby Franklin there. She put a hand over her stomach. There was already another baby to think about now. But she would never forget this one. She would come every year to see him. She would always come and think about all the poor babies of the world who died because they were ill and had no medicine.

The next year, little Elliott was born in September, and Eleanor started to smile again.

Franklin had decided to run for the New York State senate. "We need a Roosevelt back in politics," he said, grinning at Eleanor. "Now, do you care to support your husband, Mrs. Roosevelt? And come talk to the reporters?"

Eleanor blushed, but she put her hand on his arm and stood up. "I never know what to say to newspaper people," she protested.

"I only wish you had that trouble, with me," he said, smiling.

ELEANOR ROOSEVELT

The reporters crowded together in the Roosevelts' small front parlor, all talking and asking questions. "Mr. Roosevelt, what do you think of the vote for women? Would you let your wife vote?"

Grinning, he said, "No, I would not let her vote. I would insist she vote for me."

Everyone laughed, and the reporter turned to Eleanor. "And you, Mrs. Roosevelt? Do you also believe that women should vote?"

"I . . ." she glanced at Franklin, but he only waited with the others for her answer. Oh, what did she think? Had she even thought about this? Finally, she said, "I . . . well, wasn't this country founded on the right to vote?"

The reporters turned back to Franklin with other questions. Finally, Franklin ushered them out. Then he turned to Eleanor and grinned. "Now you'll have to join the National Women's Party to show that you really do support the women's vote."

"Think of It—Washington, D.C."

Frowning, Eleanor thought about this. She had been so busy with the babies—so busy with everyday life, and nothing else. She looked at Franklin. "Yes," she said. "I think you're right."

"They want you to do what?" Eleanor asked.

"Become Assistant Secretary of the Navy. Think of it, Babs—Washington, D.C. I've been hoping a spot like this would open up. That's why I worked so hard to help elect President Wilson."

She thought of the children. Baby Elliott was only two, James was six and Anna, with her shining gold hair, had turned seven. And Eleanor was expecting another baby. She thought about leaving New York for Washington. She had just got used to Franklin's political parties. She liked going to debates with him. She had her own charity work.

She looked at him now and saw the excitement in his eyes.

"I guess I'd better see about packing up the house," she said.

Grinning, Franklin lifted her up and spun her around. "That's my Babs!"

They moved to Washington D.C., bringing Anna, James and baby Elliott, and Franklin's newest black Scottish terrier.

That next August, in 1914, Eleanor had another baby, another Franklin Junior. And, an ocean away, Germany invaded France and the world went to war. But life in Washington went on with parties and a whole social whirl.

Eleanor did not like all of Franklin's friends. Louis Howe, a little man who smoked too much and looked as if he had slept in his suit, had become Franklin's advisor. He hovered near Franklin, offering advice, telling him to try new things. Eleanor watched the little man and wondered how her husband put up with him.

"That's My Babs!"

One day Louis came early for a meeting with Franklin. Eleanor had no choice but to sit with him.

"Have you ever spoken in public?" Mr. Howe asked her.

Surprised, Eleanor looked up. "I spoke at school, but nothing else."

He asked questions about her years at Allenswood. Eleanor found herself telling him about more than her school years. She talked about her ambitions from that time to teach, and do something useful.

"Would you consider speaking to a visiting group of Navy wives? Nothing formal. Just something to make them feel less lonely."

Eleanor was about to refuse, but she could still remember how lonely she had first felt in Washington. "Of course I will," she replied.

The day came for her to speak to the Navy wives, and Eleanor fussed. She put on one dress, but it looked too old-fashioned. Taking it off, she put on another. Did it look too formal? Finally, she had to leave.

Twenty women sat in chairs in a big room. Eleanor stared at the faces, her mouth dry, her mind blank. "Oh, I can't . . ." she said, turning to Louis Howe.

"Of course you can. Just keep your voice low. You squeak when you get nervous." He smiled.

Eleanor gripped her purse and strode to the front of the room. Expectant, interested faces stared at her. Eleanor remembered Margaret Dix making fun of her speeches so long ago. Clearing her throat, Eleanor started talking. She talked about her first days in Washington, how she felt swallowed up by the noise and excitement. She talked about helping to make a difference. When she finished, the ladies clapped and smiled, and crowded around her to thank her.

Eleanor turned and smiled at Louis Howe, who gave her a wink and two thumbs up.

"We're Going to War with Germany."

Franklin came into the nursery and sat down next to Eleanor. "Here you are. I wanted to tell you as soon as I heard." Frowning, he pulled off his glasses. "We're going to war with Germany, Babs."

Eleanor stopped rocking baby John. He grabbed at the beads around her neck. "Will they ask you to go?"

"My work is here with the Navy, but it may come to that," Franklin answered with a tired smile. "Uncle Teddy wants to lead his Rough Riders over there and settle everything."

"I wish he could settle it the way he did the war between Japan and Russia," Eleanor said. "But it is too far gone for anyone to talk sense, I suppose."

"President Wilson tried, but Germany refuses to stop sinking our ships."

Eleanor stared down at the gurgling baby in her lap. Thank heavens the boys were so young. Anna was almost eleven, and seemed so grown up at times. But ten-year-old James still liked to play make-believe with Elliott, who was seven, and Franklin Junior was only three.

"Well, what can I do to help?" Eleanor said, looking up from her baby and straightening her shoulders.

"Are we organized for the party the Red Cross Canteen is giving?" Mrs. Daniels asked as she walked down Pennsylvania Avenue with Eleanor.

Smiling at the older woman, Eleanor nodded. "Everything is set." She turned toward the street as an ambulance sped past. "Do you know, I so very much wanted to be in the motor corps. But I can't drive."

Mrs. Daniels laughed. "I'm surprised that stopped you. Now, what about the free yarn? Do we have volunteers to knit socks for our soldiers at the front lines?"

"But I Can't Drive."

Eleanor's smile faded.

Mrs. Daniels patted Eleanor's hand. "You're thinking of your brother Hall, aren't you? It was too bad he ran off and joined up as he did. He has a wife to think of."

"Yes, but he couldn't resist. Not with our Cousin Quentin joining on the same day. They went together." Eleanor smiled again. "They both must have memorized the eye test to pass it—their vision is so bad!"

Stopping at a street corner, Mrs. Daniels turned to Eleanor. "And Franklin? When did you last hear from him? I know Mr. Daniels hated to send him to Europe, but he needed someone who could report what the Navy needs over there."

"Mr. Daniels is Secretary of the Navy. He had every right to send Franklin to France. And Franklin is like me. He must have something useful to do. In fact, my Uncle Teddy hates being stuck here. He'd much rather contribute to the war effort."

ELEANOR ROOSEVELT

Eleanor said good-bye to Mrs. Daniels and walked home to search the mail as she did every day. Today, her search was rewarded. She found a letter from Franklin. His ship, the *Dyer*, had sailed from Brest, in France, only a few days ago. She smiled, then her hand tightened on the paper. Franklin was coming home ill.

Eleanor and her mother-in-law met Franklin's ship when it docked in New York. They took him home in an ambulance. For once, Eleanor thanked heaven for her mother-in-law's firm hand. Mrs. Roosevelt kept Franklin in bed and slowly he got well again.

By November, Franklin felt well enough to go back to Washington. They took the train, and the children came with them. Washington seemed bursting with excitement and laughter. People rushed past them. Men shouted and honked their car horns.

"It's Over."

"What is it?" Franklin asked, putting down the train window and leaning out.

"The war," a sailor yelled back. "It's over!"

Franklin turned around and wrapped Eleanor in a huge hug. "It's over, Babs. It's over!"

Tears slipped down Eleanor's face. "A year and seven months," she whispered, counting the time since President Wilson had spoken in Congress, asking for war. Eleanor hugged Franklin tightly and hoped there would never be another world war like this one.

Chapter 6

A New Beginning

Eleanor stared at the bare sticks which had once been trees. They stuck up from the ground like skeleton fingers. She was with Franklin in Europe. The government had sent him to help disarm the Navy. Eleanor had come along just to see Europe again.

Now, she wished she hadn't. The last time she had seen the Boulogne woods, there were tall, leafy trees shading green meadows and spring flowers. Looking around, she felt like crying.

Sticks Which Had Once Been Trees

"Franklin, it's awful! Four years of war. So much destruction. I wish Uncle Teddy were still alive to help put it right again." She still had trouble believing Theodore Roosevelt had died so suddenly. He had grown old, but he had never been ill.

Walking beside her, Franklin smiled. "I'm not sure Uncle Teddy would have supported Wilson's League of Nations. And that may be the only hope now to keep peace in Europe."

"Well, I shall support Wilson's League. When we get home, I'll do something," Eleanor declared.

"Would you like me to do something as well?" Franklin asked with a smile.

She looked at him. He had stopped walking and he stood staring at the pitted dirt where once a forest had stood. Then he turned to her. "I plan to run for elected office in the national elections next year. For vice president."

ELEANOR ROOSEVELT

She stared at him. She hadn't really thought about what Franklin might want to do after the war. He was still Assistant Secretary of the Navy, but she knew he had further ambitions.

Franklin grinned. "It won't be easy. I'll have to travel a lot next year. And I want you to come with me to the national convention."

Looking around her, she wondered who would continue the fight for peace and reforms with Uncle Teddy gone. She looked at Franklin. At thirty-seven, two years older than herself, he looked much older. The war and his illness had thinned him, his skin pulling tight across his cheekbones. They had five children waiting for them at home, from thirteen-year-old Anna to three-year-old John. They had a rented house in Washington that didn't seem like home, and she had hoped for a family vacation the next year.

Turning, she glanced at the battered countryside again. Well, a vacation could wait one

Splashing Out of the Surf

more year. Eleanor smiled at her husband. "I suppose that means I'll have to give speeches. Do you think Louis has time enough to work with me?"

When the election ended in the fall of 1920, Franklin's party lost to Warren G. Harding. Eleanor almost felt relieved, but she saw how disappointed Franklin looked.

Franklin said they should go to Campobello Island, in Canada, for a vacation the next summer. After spending the winter in New York, she and Franklin packed up all five children—Anna, James, Elliott, Franklin Jr. and John—and took the train north.

Summer heat sparkled on the water. Splashing out of the surf, Franklin ran over to her. He threw himself onto a towel next to her, water dripping off him. "Those children wore me out."

"The election wore you out."

He grinned. "Well, I've got a long vacation now."

Smiling, she asked, "Franklin, do you think we might finally get a home of our own?"

He looked surprised. "I'll build you one right here, if you like. We'll bake every summer . . ."

"And freeze every winter! No, thank you."

Franklin shivered. "That wind is cold. I think I'll go in and change."

Frowning, she watched him as he walked back to the house, a towel around him. It was a warm breeze that brushed her skin, but Franklin looked chilled.

The next day Franklin said his legs ached. Laying a hand on his face, Eleanor felt his hot, damp skin. He grinned and joked about it, but Eleanor didn't laugh. She made him get dressed and took him to see a doctor, as if he were no bigger than baby John.

Sitting outside Franklin's room in the hospital, Eleanor sat worrying, her purse gripped in her hands. Franklin had burned with fever all the way down to the hospital in Maine. Even

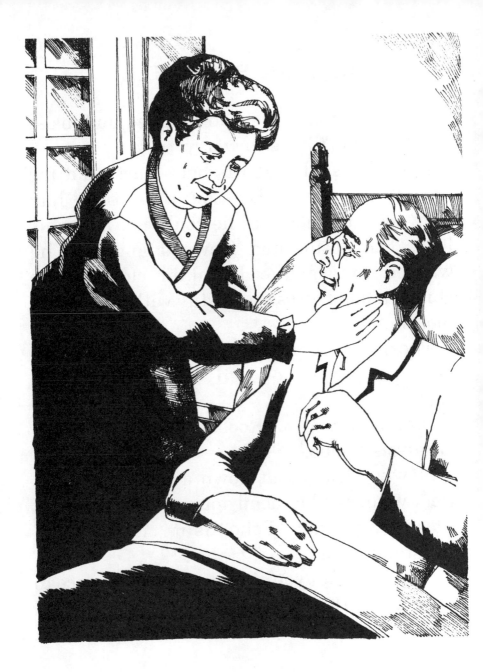

Eleanor Felt His Hot Damp Skin.

with his face pale, he had laughed and joked that she didn't have to worry.

Franklin said that his back hurt. And his hands and arms. By the time they had arrived at the hospital he could not move his legs. The doctor had frowned and said he wanted to examine Franklin closely. The children had been sent to stay with Franklin's mother.

The door opened behind her. Eleanor got up, gripping her purse even tighter. "Is he all right?"

"I'm sorry, Mrs. Roosevelt. It's infantile paralysis—polio."

Slowly, Eleanor sat down again. Her knees went weak and her head spun, and if she didn't sit she would fall. "Polio? Is it . . . is it fatal?" she stammered.

"It can be. But your husband has a chance to get better," the doctor said. "He's young. And strongwilled. He'll need rest. And quiet. I'm very sorry," he added. "But there is something else you must know. Your husband will probably not be able to leave his bed for the rest of his life."

Changes came to the New York house that Franklin's mother had built for them.

As soon as the doctor said that Franklin was over the worst and could come home, Eleanor made plans. The summer had slipped away and she had started the children back in school. She had to be strong for Franklin, for the children. If Franklin were to get better, he must believe that he *could* get better. It didn't matter if he couldn't walk, or couldn't even move his legs—he must believe that he would again someday.

Eleanor asked Louis Howe and a live-in nurse to move into the small house, making it even more crowded. Eleanor read to Franklin, and so did Louis. She clipped newspaper

"He Should Retire," Mrs. Roosevelt Said.

articles for him, rubbed his sore, stiff muscles and helped him with the exercises the doctor ordered.

Winter passed slowly, months of cold, wet snow and dark days. Some days, when Franklin could not even do his exercises, nothing would cheer him. He lay in his bed, his face turned away, saying nothing. And Eleanor wondered if she was doing the right thing.

Franklin's mother wanted them to move to the country, to Hyde Park. "He should retire and live quietly," Mrs. Roosevelt had said, her voice sharp.

Walking to her room, Eleanor crumpled onto her bed. Could she do it all? Could she be both mother and father to the children and also nurse Franklin back to health? She felt as if she had no life of her own. Franklin needed to be a part of life. She knew that. But would the rest of her life be spent looking after him?

The tears began to fall. Eleanor tried to stop them, but they poured out. She heard a sob and realized it had come from within her. Once she started crying, she couldn't stop.

Bunching into the door, the children stared at her. Louis Howe heard her sobs and tried to comfort her. She tried again to stop crying, but she couldn't. All those tears, saved up over many years, spilled out now—tears for the small hurts, and the big ones, tears for the person she had not become, tears for Franklin.

Finally, Mr. Howe left. Eleanor lay in the darkness, her sobs slowly quieting. She felt a hand slip into hers, and reached out to touch soft curls. Anna.

"Mother?"

Eleanor took a deep breath and looked up. Anna sat on the bed, her eyes worried. "Mother, are you all right?"

Anna would be eighteen soon. She would come out into society. And the boys needed

She Felt a Hand Slip into Hers.

someone, too. Sitting up, Eleanor made a sudden decision. She had to go on. But she had to have more help. She would hire assistants. She would hire secretaries to write letters and make appointments and deal with the little things of life.

That would give her time for a life of her own. She needed to put something back in her own life so that she could keep giving to her family. She had to have a life, too.

Eleanor wiped at her eyes and tried to laugh. It sounded too much like a sob, so she caught Anna in a tight hug.

"Did you like my article?" Eleanor asked, sitting next to Franklin.

The magazine crackled in his hands. He smiled. "It's wonderful, Babs. And they paid you five hundred dollars for it?"

"Yes, and asked for more. And I'm going to spend some of it on swimming lessons for myself. Someone must teach the children, after all."

He grinned. "Better add sailing to your list. The boys are mad to try it. And what about driving a car? Isn't it about time you learned to get around on your own?"

Eleanor looked at her husband. His face still seemed thin and tired. He had put on weight again, but she knew that his legs had wasted to skin and bone. She knew because she rubbed the soreness from them every night. But she liked this new look in his eyes. It was as if he'd faced the worst and had won. He couldn't walk, but he could use his hands and arms again. If he could do that much, then maybe . . .

"Very well—sailing, too. And driving and flying."

"Now, wait a minute. I didn't say anything about airplanes."

Sailing at Campobello

"But, Franklin—Amelia Earhart, the flyer, thinks I could be a first-class pilot. I've already been up once with her."

"You've been . . ." His face paled. "Eleanor, you know how dangerous I think it is to fly. Promise me you won't fly unless you must."

He seemed so worried, Eleanor gave in. "Very well—I won't fly myself. But I can't promise not to go up as a passenger."

So she went sailing instead at Campobello. She splashed with the children as Franklin used to, and wrestled with them and rode horses with them. It amazed her to find that so many of the things she had feared when she was younger had somehow lost their power over her. *Like Madeleine,* she thought, remembering her old nurse. So many things had frightened Eleanor because she had allowed them to.

Eleanor spoke quite often now for the League of Women Voters and other groups.

ELEANOR ROOSEVELT

The 19th Amendment to the Constitution had passed four years before, giving women the vote. Eleanor worked hard now for an Equal Rights Amendment for women. She spoke often about equal pay. So much work needed to be done to help people.

Then one day Franklin surprised her. He called her out onto the porch. She came out, wondering what he wanted. Slowly, he stood. He leaned heavily on a cane, but he stood on his own feet.

"Franklin!" She hurried to him, afraid he would fall, frightened that he would hurt himself.

He gripped her arm. "I've been practicing. I can walk—a little. And I'm going to speak at the Democratic convention this summer— Louis arranged it. We'll let the world know that I'm back. And then we'll see what we can do about better working conditions."

But not only Franklin spoke at the convention.

On His Own Two Feet

Standing in simmering silence, Eleanor looked at the smug male faces seated around the table. The heat of summer drew perspiration from her forehead.

"Gentlemen, it is always easier to let things go," she began. "But I care enough about this issue that I must take a stand. I came to this convention as a delegate on women's issues. It is now 1924. Women got the vote four years ago, but we have nothing to say about who is chosen as a candidate. You are the party leaders. You can change that."

The faces turned away. Eleanor had seen this at every meeting. For three months she had fought and struggled for women to be included in the primary elections for candidates. Now, these stuffy, old-fashioned men were turning their faces away yet again. They had been her last hope.

Inside her head, her temper flared higher than the hundred-degree heat in the room.

They were all so stubborn! Backward-looking and stubborn!

Standing, one of the men thanked Eleanor for coming. She heard the tone in his voice—that smug tone as if he might pat her on the head before sending her home.

She turned. At the door, she stopped and turned back. "Gentlemen," she said. "Women's issues are humanity's issues—good wages, health care and safe working conditions affect everyone. If you want the people's vote, then listen to the people."

It took every bit of Grandmother Hall's training not to slam the door behind her.

Back in the convention hall, Eleanor started toward her seat. She was angry. But she was angry mostly at herself for not doing better. She must find others who would listen—if not this election, then next. Around her, the low hum of several hundred people sounded almost like the ocean. She wished now that

Slowly They Walked to the Podium.

she were back at Campobello with the younger children.

Then she saw Franklin. He stood on one side of the stage, a crutch under one arm, and his other arm on sixteen-year-old James. Slowly, they walked to the podium. As Franklin reached the stand, he straightened and smiled. Eleanor knew that he smiled at the simple pleasure of being able to walk.

Cheering, the crowd rose. People stamped their feet and shouted. Hands clapped. Franklin raised his hand to quiet the crowd, then he began to talk. Eleanor had never heard him talk so well about the problems the country faced.

After the convention, Eleanor found Franklin to tell him how much she liked his speech. She had to wait until a crowd of men left his side, and then she moved to him and smiled.

Before she could say anything, he grinned at her. "They tell me I should think of running for Governor of New York! What do you think, Babs?"

Eleanor's heart pounded faster. Would she have to give up her work to be a governor's wife? She tried to smile. She knew how much Franklin wanted to be back in politics. What would she do?

To Be a Governor's Wife?

Chapter 7

Depression Years

"Mrs. Roosevelt, could you stand a little closer to the new Governor? Not you, Mrs. Roosevelt. Mrs. *Eleanor* Roosevelt."

Eleanor glanced at Mother Roosevelt. The older woman stiffened. "Just take the photograph, please!" she said.

Turning back, Eleanor tried to stand a little closer to her husband. Franklin looked very dashing in his new suit. He sat in a chair between Eleanor and Mother Roosevelt. He still had trouble walking, but he hated people to think of him as a cripple.

The photographer snapped the flash, and Eleanor relaxed.

Mother Roosevelt let out a sigh. "Really, Franklin, I don't know why you want me in this photograph."

He grinned at her and caught her hand. "Because I wouldn't be here without the two ladies who helped get me elected."

Mother Roosevelt glanced at Eleanor, then she smiled slightly. "If I had had my way, Franklin, you would have retired to live at Hyde Park after your illness. However, I am proud of you." She looked at Eleanor. "Both of you."

Before Eleanor could say anything, the doors opened and reporters hurried forward to ask questions.

"Mrs. Roosevelt, you wrote an article, *Women Must Learn to Play the Game as Men Do,* about women needing to get into politics. Will you do that now that your Mr. Roosevelt is governor?"

"One Politician is Enough."

She put her hand on Franklin's shoulder. "I will continue to write and work for better conditions for everyone—but I think one politician is enough in our house," she replied.

Franklin grinned. "She should be the one to run. She's popular enough to win," he said, beaming.

When the reporters finally left, Franklin turned to her. "Babs, you do need to get into politics—as my legs. I need someone who can get around and see things for me. How do you feel about touring a hospital?"

She smiled at him. "Do I have to drive myself, or do you think we can afford a driver?"

Even though Franklin told her what to ask, Eleanor walked through the hospital feeling hurried and lost. She looked into some rooms and then had to see more rooms. She patiently listened to what everyone told her, nodding and smiling and wishing Franklin were with her.

That evening, she told Franklin what she had seen.

"But did you go into the kitchen?" he asked. "Did you stir the soup to find out if they put any meat in it? Did you talk to the patients? Did you wander off to see any rooms not on the tour?"

Eleanor blinked. "Well, no. Should I have?"

"Should you? Yes! Remember when I used to inspect the battleships for the Navy? You came with me sometimes. That's how you must do these tours. Find out what they *don't* want you to see, and find out why they don't want you to see it."

The next trip—to a prison—went better. No one tried to stop Eleanor when she started walking down a hallway. If she asked questions, people tried to get answers for her. She began to enjoy these visits.

Eleanor went everywhere, to slums and banks, to hospitals and orphanages. After one

Eleanor Went Everywhere.

of her trips, she came home to find Franklin frowning at a newspaper headline.

"What is it?" she asked, hurrying to him. It couldn't be another war. Europe still had not recovered from the last one. Franklin held up the newspaper for her to read the headline.

October 24, 1929—Stock Market Crashes.

Eleanor sat down. "Have we lost our money, too?"

"Some. Like everyone else. Banks are closing. But some people lost everything. There will be a lot of people without jobs soon," Franklin told her.

Eleanor's visits started to include soup kitchens, where hungry people could eat free of charge. She liked to put on an apron and help serve the soup. It reminded her of going to the slums with her father to help the poor. She visited camps where people lived because they had lost their homes. She started sending money to anyone who wrote for help.

"Franklin," she remarked one afternoon, "I think this is the first day we've had to ourselves in a month." Eleanor turned to him. They sat on the porch of Franklin's house in the village of Hyde Park, in upstate New York.

Franklin looked up from his paper. "Is it? Well, don't blame my schedule. I'm not the one on the Women's Trade Union League, and picketing for fair wages, and . . ."

"As if you didn't encourage me. And with the children almost grown, I need to keep busy. I won't be one of those women who lives only through her children. So, I've been thinking."

He folded his paper. "That usually means you want me to do something."

She smiled. "No. Not much. I'm thinking of buying a school in New York City. A place called Todhunter. I want to start a girl's school. I've always wanted to teach."

"Don't you have enough to do?"

"When Has Anything Stopped You?"

"Be serious. Todhunter could be an excellent school and I only plan to teach part-time. And there's something else . . ." She looked at him seriously. "The stone cottage you built for me, at Val-Kill? Well, do you think I might turn it into a place where women can learn how to build furniture? A woman-run factory. There's no reason why the world shouldn't have a female Henry Ford—but women need a place to learn how to run a business."

Franklin reached over to take her hand. "Babs, when has anything I ever said stopped you from doing just as you please?"

She laughed. "I don't expect you to stop me. But you're a lawyer, and I want your advice on how best to do all this."

Eleanor bought the Todhunter school and started teaching part-time. Her friends, Marion Dickerman and Nancy Cook, ran the school. Originally Eleanor had hired them to help with letters and her schedules, but now they were friends. Without Marion and Nancy, Eleanor didn't know how she would manage her busy days.

On Monday, Tuesday and Wednesday mornings, Eleanor taught at Todhunter. In the afternoons, she met with political leaders and toured places for Franklin. Evenings meant dinners and more meetings. And she had her own family. But Eleanor had no trouble finding time for everything, because she loved it all.

Standing before her class one Monday, Eleanor thought of how much she loved her work and her life. She turned to the rows of interested young faces. "If I teach you nothing else, I want to teach you to be somebody—to be yourself. Life is meant to be lived. And your life is your own to live. And, above all, remember, your education never ends. You're never too old to learn."

"Life Is Meant To Be Lived."

Eleanor sat in her study, head low, hands gripped together. She felt lost. She felt tired.

She heard the squeak of Franklin's wheelchair. Looking up, she brushed at her eyes. She didn't want him to see her like this.

"Babs?"

She smiled at him and got up. "Is it six already? I must change if we're going out to the Junior League fundraiser. Do you think I've worn the white evening dress too much?"

"An evening dress didn't make you cry, Babs. What is it?"

She sat down again. Then she pulled out the newspaper and showed him the headlines. "Look. It's been almost three years since the Depression started, Franklin. And this emergency relief is just not enough. None of it is enough—not the charities, not the fundraisers! It's nice to hand out milk and bread—it gives you a comfortable feeling inside—but it does nothing to change the world. We need new solutions, not charity."

"I know." Slowly, Franklin got up from his wheelchair. Moving stiffly, he sat down beside her on the sofa. "I've been talking to Louis Howe and others and—Babs, I'm going to run for President this year."

She stared at him. Then she glanced around. Since Franklin was elected in 1928, they had lived nearly five years in the Governor's mansion in Albany, New York. For five years it had been home, or at least a place to stay. What would happen to Todhunter? She couldn't live in Washington and teach. And what about the factory at Val-Kill? Could it run on its own?

Franklin smiled at her and took her hands. "I need your support now, Babs."

Forcing a smile, she gripped his hands tightly. "You always have that."

But what on earth would she do if he was elected?

Her First Press Conference as First Lady

Chapter 8

First Lady

"Mrs. Roosevelt, has the President's illness changed him?"

Eleanor took a deep breath. This was her first press conference as a First Lady—the President's wife. Franklin had been elected in 1932 and had taken office the following March. In Washington, Eleanor saw how the women reporters were losing their jobs because of the Depression, so she decided to start special talks for women reporters to give them headlines that might help them keep working.

She thought about her answer. She wanted to give an honest reply.

"Yes, it has." She looked around at the faces. Some of the women looked shocked. "His illness has changed him. He understands better what it is to suffer in this life, and what it is to overcome adversity."

"Mrs. Roosevelt, what about your own efforts to win better wages for working women? Will you give up that work?"

Eleanor looked for the woman who had asked that question. Lorena Hickok, the highest paid woman reporter, waited for her answer.

"It's not only wages, Miss Hickok. It's work. The Depression is worse this year—1933—than when it started. Sixteen million Americans, one third of the people who can work—can't find jobs."

"Mrs. Roosevelt, one question every woman in the country wants to know is, how do you find time to shop for clothes?"

"Will You Give Up that Work?"

Eleanor laughed. "I'm quite happy with my ten-dollar bargain dresses, but I do love nice clothes. And I have to dress in the evening for formal events. So I have to find time for fittings here at the White House."

The questions came, fast and noisy. Eleanor still wasn't sure she liked all this attention. Finally, the hour ended. Lorena Hickok, a slim woman in a dark dress, came up to Eleanor. "This move to Washington has been hard on you, hasn't it?" she asked.

Eleanor glanced at the woman, surprised. She thought she had hidden her own fears of moving the family from New York to Washington again.

Miss Hickok smiled. "Don't worry, Mrs. Roosevelt—your answer is off the record. I won't print it.

Smiling, Eleanor relaxed. "Do you know, my grandmother would be shocked if she were alive today and could see me. She thought only bad people were ever mentioned in news-papers. And reporters were not asked into 'nice' houses, Miss Hickok."

"Call me Hick, please," the woman said, smiling. "And these days, radio is invited into everyone's house. You should think about doing some radio programs. That's the way to get the word out now."

Eleanor smiled. "I'll think about that."

The reporter smiled. Then she put out her hand to shake Eleanor's.

Fall nipped the air in West Virginia, turning the leaves orange and yellow. Eleanor walked beside two men in worn coats and steel helmets. Both men had coal-streaked faces and blackened clothes. She watched the men as they talked. It was hard to tell if either man's skin, under all the coal dust, was really light or dark.

"Mrs. Roosevelt, you're not going down there, are you?"

She Strode Toward the Entrance.

ELEANOR ROOSEVELT

Eleanor turned and smiled at the young Secret Service man. "Why shouldn't I?" Turning back, she strode toward the entrance with the miners.

Photographers followed her. She turned and smiled at them and waved, and a dozen flashes popped. The young Secret Service man stayed near her, hovering as if he thought someone planned to push Mrs. Roosevelt down the mine.

"Do I get to wear a hat like yours?" Eleanor asked, pointing to the miner's steel hat with its lamp. Quickly a hat was found to fit the First Lady.

They went down the mine shaft in a steel cage elevator. Eleanor had thought she would be frightened by looking down into the coal mine. But it was so black, with only tiny spots of light every twenty feet, that she couldn't see anything. Just black darkness. *How awful to have to work in such darkness every single day,* she thought.

When the elevator stopped, everyone stepped out into the bottom of the mine.

Water dripped from the wooden support beams. Narrow tunnels stretched into darkness. Light pooled around the small crowd at the elevator. Eleanor stared into the mine. "You work down here ten hours at a time?"

The miner who had given her the hat nodded. "Longer sometimes. The lucky ones are the ones with jobs. Some here have forgotten what it's like to get a regular paycheck."

She shook her head sadly. When they rode back up in the elevators, Eleanor turned to the miner. "Do you think I could visit with your family?"

The miner smiled. The Secret Service man frowned even more. Above ground, Eleanor followed the miner toward a wooden shack.

The Bottom of the Mine

"I've got six children," the miner said, stepping inside the shack. He pointed to six small, hungry faces. The children huddled close, but one boy ran away into the backyard.

Smiling, Eleanor bend down beside the youngest girl. "My daughter looked just like you when she was ten," she said smiling. Getting up, Eleanor noticed a small bowl of cooked meat scraps on the table. She wondered if the family had a dog. Then the miner's wife began to spoon the meat onto plates. It was the children's lunch, she realized, sadly.

Outside, the girl she had spoken to and the boy who had run out gathered by the door. The boy held something white and furry in his arms.

"Hello. What do you have?" Eleanor asked, bending down to him.

He shot his sister a scared glance, then blurted out, "Don't let 'em eat my rabbit. Don't let 'em, please?"

ELEANOR ROOSEVELT

The boy's sister pointed at the white fur. "It's his rabbit. He's scared we're gonna have to kill it and eat it."

The boy pulled his rabbit away.

Eleanor smiled and stroked the soft fur. "I'll make sure you have something better to eat than rabbit, all right?"

The young Secret Service man pulled out a ten-dollar bill and gave it to the boy. "Here, kid."

Getting up, Eleanor smiled at the Secret Service man. "Thank you so much. Now, let's go see what the President can do about better jobs for these men."

Franklin maneuvered his wheelchair into the Blue Room. "Eleanor, how would you like a trip to Puerto Rico? It may not be a state, but the people who live there are American citizens. And all I've been hearing is complaints from the sugar companies on one side, and stories of workers slaving for low wages and not enough food on the other. I want the truth."

The Papers Call Me 'Eleanor Everywhere'."

ELEANOR ROOSEVELT

Looking up from her schedule, Eleanor smiled at him. "You know that the papers are already calling me 'Eleanor Everywhere' because of all my trips."

He grinned. "Then why don't we add a lecture tour around the whole United States? I need to find out if my 'New Deal' is really making new jobs, or if it's just turning Washington upside-down."

"As long as I'm back by Christmas."

His grin widened. "Oh, you're not allowed to miss Christmas."

A few days before her lecture tour ended, Eleanor decided to make an extra stop to visit Baltimore. She called Franklin to let him know about the change.

"Eleanor? Where are you? Why aren't you back yet?"

"I'm in prison, Franklin."

She heard his deep laugh. "I'm not surprised, but what for?"

"Only for a tour. I'll be home a day later than I'd thought."

"Well, do your best to break out, Babs. And if you can't, I'll send you a set of keys as your present this year."

Eleanor got back to the White House on Christmas Eve. She came into the house quietly. She gave her coat to a member of the staff and put her finger to her lips to signal quiet. Then she tiptoed into the drawing room.

Franklin sat near the fire, a book open on his lap. Anna sat near him, and her husband stood across the room. The boys sprawled on chairs or the floor, all looking much younger than they were.

"I am the Ghost of Christmas Past," Franklin said, acting out Charles Dickens's words.

Eleanor smiled. The clock on the fireplace mantel chimed. Soon Franklin would be toasting a new year: *To 1936, and to the United*

She Tiptoed In.

States of America, saying the words in such a way that she always felt the beginning of tears sting her eyes. These were tears of pride, for him and for her country. It would be an election year, this new year, which meant hard work and train trips criss-crossing the nation. But tonight, she had time simply to enjoy her family.

Franklin won reelection, and Eleanor settled into another four years at the White House.

"What's my schedule today?" Eleanor asked Lorena Hickok. The reporter had left her job for a new one—as Eleanor's assistant. Now, Eleanor wondered how she had ever gotten along without Hick's skills. She knew just how to handle everything, and all with a smile or a joke.

"After breakfast with the President, you have several meetings. And this afternoon is your garden party for the reform-school girls."

Hick looked up from her notepad. "Umm, Mrs. Roosevelt, some of the President's men... well, they asked if you knew that some of these girls—well, they're not white. They're worried about you getting bad press in some parts of the country."

Eleanor looked up. "For what? For having girls to a party?" She frowned, annoyed that some people were so prejudiced. Then she smiled. "If any of Franklin's advisors has a problem, he can take it up with the President."

Hick grinned. "You know he won't object."

"Of course not. No one with any sense would. Now, what else do we have to do today? Are the plans made for the annual Easter Egg Hunt?"

Three days before the Fourth of July on a sticky hot day, Eleanor dressed to greet the crown prince and princess of Sweden. Hick

She Had Felt Like a Nobody.

popped in and out of Eleanor's room, worried about schedules and what to do.

"Oh, Hick, will you stop fussing? They're just people!" Eleanor laughed, smoothing her evening dress.

Hick shook her head. "That's fine for you to say. You're the President's wife. I'm nobody. And I don't know anything about royalty!"

Eleanor laughed again. She remembered so well how she had felt like a nobody so many years ago in New York society. "With England and France at war with Germany, I don't think it's just a vacation for the Swedish prince and princess. And we've got the crown prince of Denmark and several leaders from South America and even the King and Queen of England wanting to visit next spring!"

"Yes, they all want us to help with the war," Hick replied. "We can only hope that it ends soon and that we can stay out of it this time."

With Hick's help, Eleanor held parties for royal visitor after royal visitor.

Eleanor liked King George VI, and his wife, Queen Elizabeth, a small, dainty woman. Eleanor felt sorry for all the royals; the press was always watching them. In February of 1941, the Grand Duchess of Luxembourg came to visit. And then more dukes and duchesses and prime ministers came to Washington. Everyone talked of the battles, of the cities bombed and the need to end the war.

Then in September, family matters overtook world affairs. Sara Roosevelt died on the 7th, and on that very day, Eleanor's beloved brother Hall took sick, dying two weeks later. Eleanor grieved privately over their deaths, trying to balance her sorrow with the urgent needs that pressed on her every day. The war in Europe was getting worse.

Eleanor Roosevelt worked hard for peace, but it was hard not to take sides. She talked

Royal Visitor After Royal Visitor

with the White House visitors and heard what Adolph Hitler had done to his own country—Germany—and to the countries Germany had invaded. Elliott and Franklin Junior both joined the Army. Eleanor worried that they might soon be called to fight.

Then, on December 7, 1941, as she and Franklin were having lunch, a man rushed into the room and gave Franklin a message. The President took off his glasses and read quietly. Eleanor waited.

Franklin looked up. "Babs—it's bad. Japan has flown over Hawaii and bombed Pearl Harbor. A surprise attack. They side with Germany and Italy. We'll have to fight all three. It's world war again."

Chapter 9

War Hardships

Suddenly, the White House was the center of the world. Men in suits and uniforms hurried in and out. In late December, just before Christmas, Franklin told Eleanor that Winston Churchill, the Prime Minister of England, would arrive for a visit.

"He called as soon as he heard about Pearl Harbor, but it's been top secret as to when he would arrive. And I have to meet the Russian ambassador, the Chinese ambassador, and the Dutch minister that same day."

"Would Mr. Churchill Like Tea?"

Head spinning, Eleanor listened. So much to do. She had just agreed to help with the Civilian Defense Control, and now all these visits. But she only smiled at Franklin. "Do you think Mr. Churchill would like tea when he comes, or something a little stronger?"

Eleanor found Mr. Churchill to be a short man who liked cigars and blunt language. She did not like that he kept Franklin up late in the evenings, talking about the war. Franklin looked tired. Eleanor worried that he was working too hard.

In the following year, even more royal visitors arrived at the White House. U.S. troops went to England to get ready to invade North Africa, where the British and Americans would fight the Germans.

Because of that, Franklin asked Eleanor to go to England. "You could take our boys a message from me," he said.

ELEANOR ROOSEVELT

Nervous, she thought about how dangerous the trip to England would be. But at least she would have Elliott with her. His unit had been sent to England.

"Oh, why did I let your father talk me into this trip, Elliot?" Eleanor said on their journey to London.

Elliott smiled at her. "Mother, you've already met King George and his wife. You can't still be worried."

She leaned back in her seat. "But I'm not here just as myself. I'm here representing our country."

The King and Queen met Eleanor and her son at the train station. A red carpet had been rolled out. They met so many officials that Eleanor's hand got sore from everyone shaking it.

The next day, Eleanor started her tours. Her days began at eight in the morning and ended at midnight. She visited streets destroyed by

A Red Carpet Had Been Rolled Out.

German bombs and talked to women and children. And she wrote articles about each trip. Eleanor thought sometimes about how shy she had felt when she had first come to England, to Allenswood. But she didn't feel shy now. She loved meeting all kinds of people. She met women who worked in hospitals, who drove ambulances, who ran factories. Everyone seemed so cheerful. They didn't even seem to notice the wail of air-raid sirens, a sound that made Eleanor jump.

She also went to American camps and met the servicemen. Almost every soldier had a letter he wanted sent home, so Eleanor began taking them and stuffing them in her purse, promising to mail each letter when she got back to the States.

Before she left, Mrs. Roosevelt had dinner with Prime Minister Churchill, his wife and the American ambassador. Dinner went well until Mr. Churchill asked if the U.S. supported Spain's Loyalist government.

"I think we're doing too little too late," Eleanor said. "I wish we had done more sooner."

"Mrs. Roosevelt, you and I would be the first people to lose our heads if the Loyalists had won in Spain."

"That's not important. What is important is personal freedom, and I don't think Spain will have much of that under Generalissimo Franco."

Mrs. Churchill leaned closer to her husband. "I think perhaps Mrs. Roosevelt is right," she told him.

Churchill frowned. "I have held certain beliefs for sixty years and I'm not going to change now."

Eleanor smiled. "But, Mr. Churchill, the world is changing. And we must change with it or be swept aside as antiques."

Finally, Franklin sent her a message: *I don't care how you get here, just come home.*

Franklin Junior's Ship Had Been Bombed.

ELEANOR ROOSEVELT

Eleanor got back to kisses and hugs from her family. She was so glad to be home again. But then she heard that Franklin Junior's ship had been bombed.

"Is he hurt?" she asked Franklin when she heard the news.

He frowned and shook his head. "I don't know. All we heard is that his ship made it back to a harbor for repairs."

A telegram arrived the next day, saying that Franklin Junior had been hit but he would get better, and that he had saved another boy's life. Putting down the telegram, Eleanor covered her eyes. *Every mother with a boy in the service must feel this way,* she thought.

Getting up, she pulled out the letters she'd carried home from the boys in England. Then she sat down to write a personal note to mail with each letter.

The war continued as American and British forces pushed into North Africa and then invaded Italy, Germany's ally. In the Pacific, the Americans fought bravely against Japan. Like everyone, Eleanor read the papers and listened to the news reports. She also kept up her travels in the U.S., visiting training camps and factories. No one thought about the Depression now. There was work for everyone—more than enough.

Over a quiet dinner one evening, Franklin talked about the war in the Pacific. "I'm worried that our allies in New Zealand and Australia feel that we don't think about them. I want to let them know that we know they're important to this war effort. Do you think you could manage a goodwill trip there, Babs?"

Eleanor thought about it, then said, "Of course, but I want to visit our troops in the Pacific, too."

Franklin smiled. "Then you'd better buy yourself a uniform. I'll see what I can arrange in the way of military flights."

"I Want to Visit Our Pacific Troops Too."

ELEANOR ROOSEVELT

Flying across the Pacific, Eleanor wondered how the pilot could see any dot of land in the vast, blue water. She bit her lip as the plane dropped. Would the plane land in the ocean? Suddenly, land rose up under the wheels in a flash of tan sand. She let out a breath of air. They had landed safely. She got up. Her feet felt numb from the long flight from Hawaii, but now, here she was on Christmas Island.

The men seemed eager to greet Mrs. Roosevelt, with big smiles and warm handshakes. Eleanor felt ready to melt in the heat, but soon she was in a jeep, bouncing over dirt roads to her room.

When she walked inside, she almost screamed. Tiny red bugs swarmed over the floor and walls. She backed up a step. Holding her breath, she looked behind her. She couldn't scream. What would everyone think if she did? So she stamped hard on the floor. "Shoo! Get!" The red bugs scurried away. Stepping into her room, Eleanor wondered what else she'd find.

Eleanor soon learned that rats, snakes and bugs were the biggest problem on every Pacific island. And the heat! She wrote home to Franklin, thanking him for telling her to buy herself thin cotton uniforms. And she listened to her son's advice that she talk to the noncommissioned officers and the enlisted men.

On the island Noumea, Eleanor met Admiral Halsey. He didn't smile at her when she stepped off the plane. Eleanor walked around the naval base and then asked, "May I go to Guadalcanal, Admiral?"

He frowned at her. "There's still fighting there."

"I won't go if you think it isn't safe, but I would like to see the boys and let them know how everyone back home supports them." She gave the admiral her warmest smile.

Eleanor Met With Maori People.

He looked away, frowned, then nodded, scowling even more. "Well, go to New Zealand and Australia first. I'll make my decision about Guadalcanal later."

In New Zealand, Eleanor met with the native Maori people as well as with government officials. She gave speeches in Australia and visited Red Cross hospitals.

By the time Eleanor got back to Noumea, Admiral Halsey met her with smiles. "I've been hearing good reports. Your visit has done a lot to improve our military morale. Do you still want to go to Guadalcanal?"

The next morning at six A.M., Eleanor was on yet another flight over white-tipped waves.

Army officers met her plane at the dirt air field on Guadalcanal. They drove her around the island, and then to a small cemetery.

"The local people built this church for us," one officer said.

ELEANOR ROOSEVELT

Eleanor got out of the jeep. Walking around the lush, tropical foliage of the cemetery, she stopped to read the crosses in the ground. Some had the Star of David carved into the wood. Some had simple words. She stopped at a cross near the church. A battle-scarred helmet hung on the white wood.

Best buddy ever.

Simple words—words from the heart. She wiped a tear from the corner of her eye. There must never be another war like this. She promised herself that when this war ended, she would do everything she could to make sure of that.

"Franklin, do you feel well?" Eleanor touched his head. It felt hot.

"It's just a fever. Too much work, I guess." The President smiled, but he looked tired. "It's been a busy year, this 1945—the Yalta conference, then the invasion of France in June, and then the reelection. This is going to be my last

Best Buddy Ever

term, Babs. We'll retire to Hyde Park when my fourth term is up."

Eleanor frowned and covered his hand with her own. His skin felt so thin and dry, as if he'd been used up. "Will you at least go to Warm Springs for some rest?"

Franklin smiled. "I'll go this April. Do you want to come to Georgia with me? We'll make it a vacation."

"Oh, Franklin, I can't. I've promised to stay for a charity dinner at the Sulgrave Club. I suppose I can put it off."

"No, Babs, you stay. Your work is important." He winked at her. "Besides, that way you can take the train down after the dinner and bring me all the latest Washington gossip."

Eleanor stayed in Washington for the thrift-shop benefit at the Sulgrave. Halfway through the evening, a quiet young Secret Service man told her that a phone call had come for her and that she must leave for the White House immediatley.

She looked up at him, her hands turning cold. She had seen that look before—always in the faces of people with bad news.

Something had happened to Franklin.

Getting up, she hurried out. In the car to the White House, she sat with both hands clenched in her lap.

At the White House, one of Franklin's assistants met her. "I'm sorry, Mrs. Roosevelt. We just got word. The President died today."

Eleanor sat down. Such a lovely April day. April 12th. And Franklin had been looking forward to retiring to Hyde Park after this term. He hadn't even seen the end of the war. She wanted to cry, but she couldn't. Not with so much to do. She loosened her grip on her chair and tried to think of what to do. "You had better send for Vice President Truman," she said.

"Is There Anything We Can Do for *You*?"

When Harry Truman arrived, he hurried to her. Eleanor still sat in the same chair. Her purse lay in her lap. She kept thinking how confused Franklin's dog, Fala, would be without his master around.

"Is there anything we can do for you?" Truman asked.

Eleanor looked at him and blinked. "Is there anything we can do for *you?* You're the one we must pray for now—Mr. President."

Chapter 10

Ambassador to the World

Eleanor remembered Queen Victoria's funeral as the procession for Franklin's funeral moved slowly through the streets of Washington. The men on horseback . . . the carriages . . . the crowds in black . . . and the quiet. Many people cried.

She wore black. Anna walked beside her. None of it seemed real. She thought of it as another state ceremony, but not as Franklin's funeral. She had so many things to ask him. A joke to share. A story to tell. She missed him so much already.

She Missed Him So Much Already.

After the service, she and Anna took the train to Hyde Park. She remembered how she had met Franklin on a train so long ago. He was going home to Hyde Park now—to his rose garden. She stared out at the darkness.

They buried Franklin, and Eleanor dedicated a memorial in the library built in his name at Hyde Park. Eleanor was sitting next to his marble monument. Fala, Franklin's black Scottish Terrier, lay at her feet, his head on his paws. Fala missed Franklin.

So many people were so saddened now that he was gone. The war had ended in September, but even that good news did not remove this shadow.

What was she to do now? She still had her writing and her charities. But it didn't seem enough, somehow.

She thought of Val-Kill.

Years ago, Franklin had built the stone cottage for her beside the Val-Kill stream on his Hyde Park land. He had had such fun building her the cottage. Val-Kill still housed her furniture factory, but now it didn't need her. It was running well without her.

A tear escaped the corner of her eye. Should she stay at Val-Kill? She had grandchildren nearby. She loved to visit them. But a visit could only last a few weeks. And she did not want to live through her children and grandchildren.

Should she travel? Would that help?

She had been to Europe with the boys to see the destruction left by the war. So much was gone. They had stopped at the muddy ruins of a place called Zilcheim. She had seen an old woman dressed in black, crying beside the stone rubble that had once been a house.

The woman had looked up and pulled back the sleeve of her dress. She had held out her wrinkled arm for Eleanor to see the numbers tattooed in blue on her skin—numbers from a concentration camp.

Numbers from a Concentration Camp

"Israel. Israel," the woman had said softly.

Eleanor had watched the woman and realized what that small portion of land must mean to someone who had been through the worst of the war. Israel—a place where one could be safe. All over Europe, the roads were filled with refugees from many countries, trying to find their way back from the ruins. So many people needed homes now.

Then Eleanor thought of the phone call she had gotten from President Truman.

"The first meeting of the United Nations is going to be held in London, starting in January this next year. I want you to serve as one of the U.S. delegates."

"It's impossible," she'd said. "How can I help organize the United Nations when I have no background or training as a diplomat?"

He laughed. "What do you think you've been doing flying around the world these last few years and meeting with other world leaders?"

ELEANOR ROOSEVELT

Eleanor thought about that now. She wondered what Franklin would have told her to do—but she knew.

"Ambassador to the World," President Truman had called her. There was so much to do. The Soviet Union was creating a new kind of war—the Cold War-long-term ill-will between Communists and the free world. Europe had to be rebuilt. So many people had been killed, cities destroyed, countries on the verge of ruin—so much had to be done. No war should ever be permitted there again.

Inside, Eleanor still felt like that little girl with the long legs and a plain face. But she knew she had other skills now. And she still had books she wanted to write—things to tell people. She wanted to appear on this new invention, called television, and talk to people about the importance of useful lives, of not giving up, and of building a better tomorrow.

"Ambassador to the World"

She looked down at Fala and smiled. "Come on, Fala. We'd better get going. There's still a lot we can do."

In her hotel room in London, Eleanor paced across the floor. "I feel like I'm walking on eggs," she said. "I'm the only woman delegate to the UN from the United States, and everyone is waiting for me to slip up."

Durward Sandifer, Eleanor's adviser, smiled. "Well, you've done more to get everyone talking than anyone else," he told her. "Your little 'after-hour' parties are known now as the only place where anything gets done."

Eleanor smiled. "Everyone gets too stuffy in regular sessions," she said. "But, this refugee issue—why is everyone ignoring it? Thousands, even millions, suffer while we just talk!

"Well, I'm going to push for a Human Rights Commission and a International Bill of Rights," Eleanor went on. "The world must learn to recognize and respect the rights of individuals if it's ever to stop war."

Eleanor kept busy drafting articles for the International Bill of Rights. She had heard that some U.S. senators thought that she had been given her position just because she was Franklin's widow. She was going to prove them wrong.

As she worked, she spoke to leaders from India and South America. With their help, she could pass her resolution. Finally, all her work ended at a UN meeting in Paris in 1948.

"We are here," Eleanor said, looking out at the leaders from all over the world, "to devise ways of safeguarding human rights. We are not here to attack each other's governments. And now I extend to you the hand of friendship and cooperation."

The delegates argued over details, but when the time came, no one voted against the International Bill of Rights. Afterward, Senator

No One Voted Against the Bill of Rights.

Arthur Vandenberg came up to Eleanor. "Do you know, I did all I could to keep you off the United States delegation," he told her. "But I have to tell you—now that I've worked with you, I'd be happy to work with you again. Anytime." He held out his hand and smiled.

Eleanor smiled in return. "I don't know anything that could make me feel less tired," she answered.

Durward Sandifer watched Eleanor pack, his narrow face pulled into a scowl. "I don't care if a Republican just got elected to the Presidency. He's an idiot not to keep you on."

Eleanor laughed. "No, Eisenhower is smart enough to know that he needs a Republican appointee at the U.N. Besides, one doesn't turn down an invitation from the prime minister of India to visit his country. So, as Mr. Nehru is kind enough to invite me to India, I am happy to go. I don't have to be in the U.N. to work for peace."

ELEANOR ROOSEVELT

"I'll miss you," Durward said, scowling even more.

"And I'll miss you. We've worked well together for almost seven years, since 1947. But I'll send you a postcard from every country."

Eleanor kept her word. She sent postcards to Durward and gifts to her grandchildren from Syria, Lebanon and Israel. Wherever she went, she visited hospitals and always asked about the children's care. In India, Eleanor talked with Prime Minister Nehru about problems of water pollution and overpopulation. She also asked about the possibility of women taking leadership positions.

In Japan, Eleanor traveled to Hiroshima. During President Truman's administration, the United States had dropped the atomic bomb on Hiroshima. Walking through the city now, Eleanor was relieved that Franklin had not been the one to have had to make that difficult decision. She stopped near the bomb

She Sent Postcards and Gifts.

crater where a memorial park was being built. Grass had begun to push up through the barren ground.

God grant to men greater wisdom in the future, Eleanor thought.

In the spring of 1957, the *New York Post* asked Eleanor to go to Russia and write a series of articles on the country. It took months for Eleanor to get permission to travel there.

"Does everyone think I'll come home a Communist?" Eleanor asked her daughter Anna one day.

Anna laughed. "No, Mother. I'm sure they think you'll topple the Russian government!"

As soon as Eleanor landed in Moscow she asked for an interview with the Russian leader, Nikita Khrushchev. Waiting in a garden, she turned and saw a short, bald-headed man with a wide smile. "Mr. Khrushchev?" she asked, addressing him.

He smiled more and said something in Russian. Then another man turned and said to Eleanor in English, "Mr. Khrushchev is delighted to meet you. He remembers President Roosevelt as a great man."

Eleanor smiled and pulled out a notepad. "The war was over ten years ago, yet Russia doesn't disarm. Why not?" she asked.

"When we increase our arms it is because of your troops in Europe," Mr. Khrushchev answered through his interpreter.

"If there is fear on both sides, then shouldn't we work to build confidence, perhaps by exchanging ideas?" Eleanor said then.

The Russian leader smiled and nodded as he listened to the translator. "Perhaps we can. At least *we* can talk without shooting at each other, and that is a little progress."

Stepping out of the Broadway theater, Eleanor turned to her daughter. "Do you know, Anna—I thought I wouldn't like the

"I Thought I Wouldn't Like the Play."

play, but I did. And what a nice title—
Sunrise at Campobello."

Anna tilted her head and looked at her
mother. "Was Father's being stricken with
polio anything like the play?"

Eleanor smiled. "No . . . well, they got the
Louis Howe character right. But their Eleanor
didn't seem like me at all."

"Well, I hope, at seventy-five, you're finally
going to slow down some," Anna said.

"But I've planned to do a program on
refugee stories. And not only is 1960 Refugee
Year for the U.N.—it's also an election year for
our next president."

"The boys are backing Senator Kennedy,
you know, Mother."

Eleanor laughed. "Then it would be point-
less for me to oppose them, wouldn't it? I do
hope I can help."

"Mother, after the election, you really must
slow down."

Eleanor got into a taxi with her daughter. She reached over and patted Anna's hand. "After the election, I will. But just now there is so much to do, so many challenges, so many needs, so much that is profoundly interesting."

"Such as your home, and your grandchildren?" Anna asked, smiling.

In the dark cab, Eleanor turned and looked at the glittering lights of New York. "Do you know, darling," she remarked. "Your father gave me Val-Kill as a home. But I had a home all along. The whole world was always my real home."

"The World Was Always My Home."

"The world was always his home..."